SHOPPING FOR FOOD AND DRINK
in Northern France and Belgium

Damse Vaarte canal, near Brugge

HOPPING FOR FOOD AND DRINK
in Northern France and Belgium

BY
MARC AND KIM MILLON

PHOTOGRAPHS BY
KIM MILLON

To Guy

BY THE SAME AUTHORS

The Wine & Food of Europe
The Wine Roads of Europe
The Taste of Britain
The Wine Roads of France
Flavours of Korea
The Wine Roads of Italy
The Wine Roads of Spain

Front cover: Philippe Olivier, Boulogne-sur-Mer
Back cover: *Pâtisseries*

First published in Great Britain in 1994 by PAVILION BOOKS LIMITED, 26 Upper Ground, London SE1 9PD

Text copyright © Marc Millon 1994   Photographs copyright © Kim Millon 1994

Designed by John Youé and Alan Grant

The moral right of the authors has been asserted

A CIP catalogue record for this book is available from the British Library

ISBN 1 85793 147 5

Printed and bound in Great Britain by Butler and Tanner Ltd, Frome and London

2 4 6 8 10 9 7 5 3 1

This book may be ordered by post direct from the publisher. Please contact the Marketing Department. But try your bookshop first.

Eurotunnel would like to point out that the views of the publisher and authors of this book are not necessarily those of Eurotunnel.
Le Shuttle is a trademark of Eurotunnel.

CONTENTS

INTRODUCTION

**Le Tunnel sous La Manche est arrivé !
Profitons-en !**
One of the most compelling motives
for a short cross-Channel break is
undoubtedly the unrivalled food and
drink shopping opportunities available
on the other side. Throughout
northern France and Belgium, from
even the smallest villages to the major
cities, the selection of fine produce,
products and prepared foods on
display is literally mouthwatering:
twice-a-day baked breads, *croissants*
and colourfully glazed fruit *pâtisseries*;
a profusion of delicious pork products
from *maître charcutiers*, including
regional *pâtés*, *terrines*, *rillettes*, *saucisses*,
boudins, *andouillettes* and hams, as well
as delicious dish-of-the-day *plats
cuisinés*; countless luscious farmhouse
cheeses, many only available locally
and made from unpasteurized *lait cru*;
superlative seasonal fruits and
vegetables; shellfish and seafood along
the coast; the greatest beers in the
world from Belgium; chocolates
galore, as well as scores of delightful
local and regional sweets; Champagnes
from growers and *grandes marques*
alike; and, of course, a selection of
outstanding vintage, as well as lesser
known but equally drinkable and
inexpensive, country wines.

There has never been a better time
to visit northern France and Belgium
on a food and drink shopping spree.
Eurotunnel's Le Shuttle quite simply
revolutionizes cross-Channel travel.
Passage between Britain and France
now takes just thirty-five minutes,
platform to platform, in passenger
vehicle shuttles. For those who prefer
not to take their own vehicles, new,
high-speed Eurostar passenger train
services pass directly through the
Channel Tunnel, connecting London
with Paris in about three hours and
London with Brussels in over three
hours. Some Eurostar trains will stop
at Calais-Fréthun which connects with
lines to Boulogne and Dunkerque, while
others will stop at the new purpose-
built Lille-Europe station. For further
information telephone the Eurostar
Information Line (0233) 361 7575.

The ease of travel coupled with the
speed and comfort of Le Shuttle
means that it has now become an
entirely feasible and, indeed, highly
enjoyable proposition simply to go
across to Calais, Boulogne or Brugge
to stock up monthly on wines and
beers, or to strike out into the
hinterland in search of a wealth of fine
farmhouse produce, tasted and
purchased direct at the source.

Pâtisseries

Shopping for Food and Drink

Moreover, not only does the ease of travel by way of the Channel Tunnel make such a journey easy and effortless, but the completion of the EC Single Market on 1 January 1993, virtually eliminating at a single stroke trade barriers between member states, makes it imperative. For, as individual travellers, we can now bring back for our own personal use unlimited quantities of goods purchased duty-paid in France, Belgium, or other EC member states, subject to the generous guidelines outlined below.

So significant are the dual benefits of the Channel Tunnel and the EC Single Market that we conjecture that food and drink shopping trips to France and Belgium are set now to become something of a mainstream activity. Even bearing in mind the cost of the cross-Channel fare, the savings on wine alone can virtually pay for a weekend break, including accommodation and meals! It is no wonder, then, that experts predict that, in the next twenty years, cross-Channel traffic will more than double.

Le Shuttle Hinterland: A Wealth of Fine Things to Eat and Drink

Because northern France and Belgium have, since Roman days at least, served as something of a continental crossroads, the people here are well used to catering to the passing hoardes, some of which have stopped for a while en route to or from elsewhere. If, historically, they prospered as traders through the centuries-long interchange and flow of people and goods, today the people of northern France and Belgium are well versed in catering to the needs of passing visitors. Consequently, there is certainly no shortage of outlets for anything you might require, not least, food and drink.

Moreover, the hinterland, extending from Calais in a radius of approximately 250–300 kilometres, is particularly – if perhaps unexpectedly – rich in a wealth of fine food and drink. Even the smallest villages and towns have a range of superlative and individual artisan *charcuteries*, *pâtisseries*, *fromageries*, *boucheries*, *épiceries* and *poissonneries*. Sniff out these small, individual shops, see and taste what they have to offer. It really is almost impossible to go too far wrong.

Throughout northern France and Belgium there are scores of weekly markets, only some of which may be worth a special visit in themselves

Dieppe market

LE SHUTTLE'S TRANSPORT SERVICE

Eurotunnel's cross-Channel Le Shuttle services operate on a turn-up-and-go basis, regardless of sea conditions, twenty-four hours a day, every single day of the year, between terminals at Folkestone and Calais. Passenger vehicle shuttles carry cars, coaches and motorcycles in either single- or double-deck carriages, depending on the height of the vehicle. Separate freight shuttles carry lorries.

Once fully operational there will be up to four passenger vehicle shuttle departures per hour during peak periods. Even during the quietest periods of the night, there will always be a minimum of one departure per hour.

How to use Le Shuttle

1. Exit the M20 motorway at junction 11a straight into the Folkestone terminal. At the toll booth, purchase your ticket by cash, credit card or cheque. Tickets can also be bought in advance from travel agents or from Le Shuttle Customer Service Centre at Cheriton Parc, Folkestone, telephone (0303) 271100.
2. After passing the toll booth, you can visit the passenger terminal where you will find duty-free and bureau de change facilities as well as restaurants and shops. Alternatively, you can head directly for Le Shuttle.
3. Pass through British and French frontier controls. Both frontier controls are situated at the departure terminal only. On the other side of the Channel, you drive directly off Le Shuttle and straight on to the motorway without further frontier controls.
4. Head for the allocation area where you wait to drive on to Le Shuttle. Attendants will direct you down the loading ramp and on board. Drive through the carriages until an attendant directs you to stop.
5. Turn the engine off and put the handbrake on. Loading takes about eight minutes and then Le Shuttle departs. During the short, 35-minute journey, you remain with your car inside the spacious, well-lit, air-conditioned carriage. Stay in your car and relax, perhaps tune into Le Shuttle radio. However, you can get out of your car to stretch your legs.
6. On arrival at Calais, attendants will direct you to drive to the front of Le Shuttle and out on to the exit ramp. This leads straight to the exit road and on to the motorway network. There are no further controls and, just over sixty minutes after leaving the motorway in Kent, you are heading off into France. Remember to drive on the right!
7. On the way home, leave the A16 *autoroute* at junction 13 which leads directly to the Calais terminal. From here, you repeat the process described above.

(such as the Saturday market at Dieppe, one of the great markets of France). Yet all of them serve the needs of the local inhabitants, purveying fresh fruit and vegetables (often from local farmhouse sources), regional *charcuterie*, local cheeses and much else. Markets are always fruitful, colourful sources of fine food and drink, and are certainly worth visiting whenever you happen to come across one.

Shopping for Food and Drink

In addition to individual shops and local markets, one of the most enjoyable aspects of food and drink shopping in northern France and Belgium is the chance to track down a local speciality, produce or product direct at the source, often direct at the farm or outlet where it is made. There are countless opportunities for such *vente directe*, often combined with tours of facilities, explanations of processes, and generous free tastings: from farmhouse cheeses to *foie gras de canard*, from growers' Champagnes to farm-distilled Calvados, from beers purchased from Trappist monks to handmade Belgian chocolates, and from fresh fish soups straight from the cauldron to plaited, bronze strings of garlic still warm from the smokehouse.

Readers' Assistance

We are certain that in the course of serendipitous food and drink wanderings, you, like us, will discover many fine and wonderful places. Any guide book, of course, is a personal selection, not a comprehensive directory and there are bound to be many worthy establishments that have not been included. We would like to appeal for your help. At the back of this book, you will find a Comment Form, together with a freepost address. We would greatly appreciate it if you would use this to make a report of food and drink establishments or other outlets (shops, farms, breweries and wine producers) that you have encountered, together with your comments on both the quality of the

Part of the Calais hinterland

LE SHUTTLE HOLIDAYS

Le Shuttle Holidays, Eurotunnel's tour-operating division, offers an attractive range of breaks, combining pre-booked accommodation with a return trip on Le Shuttle. For further information, and to obtain a copy of Le Shuttle Holidays' Breaks brochure, visit your local travel agent or telephone (0303) 271717.

produce and/or products, as well as the welcome that you received. Furthermore, we would also appreciate it if you could use the same form (photocopy if necessary) to recommend any good small hotels, restaurants, *chambres d'hôtes* or *fermes auberges* that you have visited.

Le Shuttle Small Hotels & Restaurants

While some people may cross over to France or Belgium to stock up on food and drink on a day trip, others may stock up on their return journey from a holiday elsewhere. We think that this activity is a worthy and enjoyable diversion in itself and certainly worth taking a few days over in order to enjoy at a leisurely pace. Why not, then, combine shopping for food and drink with a short break in the region? This book is intended to be used in conjunction with its companion volume, *Le Shuttle Small Hotels and Restaurants*, which covers scores of small hotels, restaurants, *fermes auberges* (farmhouse restaurants which are often themselves the source of superlative produce or products), and *chambres d'hôtes* throughout the same regions. The 🏨 symbol indicates that a town is listed in *Le Shuttle Small Hotels and Restaurants*. All towns are listed with their French or Belgian postal codes (the numbers preceding the town names).

Profitons-en !

The dual opportunities created by the Channel Tunnel and the completion of the EC Single Market are immense and exciting. Let's all *profiter* – take advantage – of the chance to get to know some wonderful places literally on our own doorstep. Whether you enjoy seeking out the best specialist shops in this book, visiting Champagne growers and sampling those great wines at the source, sharing beers with Trappist monks, inhaling the over-powering pungency of a *cave d'affinage* where great cheeses are left to mature and develop, or seeking out and indulging in a selection of the finest Belgian pralines, one thing is certain: there is indeed a wealth of outstanding food and drink shopping opportunities just across the Channel for us all to enjoy. *Profitons-en !*

November 1993
Topsham, Devon

WINE, BEER AND OTHER DRINK

Wine: The Opportunity to Make Substantial Savings

The most obvious and immediate benefit of the EC Single Market is that, as private individuals, we may now bring back large quantities of duty-paid wine and other alcoholic beverages from other member states. Minimum guideline amounts have been established and, provided these are not exceeded, there is no liability for British excise duty or VAT.

The minimum guideline amounts currently stand at 90 litres of table wines (of which 60 litres may be sparkling), 20 litres of fortified wines, 10 litres of spirits, and 110 litres of beer. It may even be possible to exceed these already generous amounts, provided you can convince HM Customs & Excise officers that the amount you are bringing back really is only for your own personal use. Considerable savings can clearly result.

For example, at present excise duty and VAT account for about £1.10 on the price of a standard bottle of average table wine purchased in the UK. By taking advantage of personal import allowances between member states, you can make a minimum saving of about £13 per twelve-bottle case. If you were to import the entire individual guideline allowance of 90 litres or 120 bottles, this represents a saving of about £130 per person. The saving on sparkling wines is even greater. Indeed, as perceived luxury

goods, Champagne and other sparkling wines attract a levy of around £1.85 per bottle, including excise duty and VAT. If purchased in France, therefore, this can amount to a saving of over £22 per twelve-bottle case, which translates, should you bring in your full 60-litre or eighty-bottle guideline allowance, to around £150. Clearly, if you have a wedding or a large party coming up, or if you simply enjoy drinking wine regularly, it is more than worthwhile crossing the Channel to stock up.

What to Buy, Where to Buy

In the not so distant days when there were green and red channels and we were only allowed to bring in about 8 litres of duty-paid table wine or eleven bottles per person without liability for British excise duty and VAT, it did not matter awfully if the few cases we purchased at the *hypermarché* before catching the ferry home were world-beaters or not. At best they could prolong the savour of a good holiday by a few weeks; at worst, they could always be used for cooking.

However, now that we are able to purchase and bring back such large quantities of wine, it should be imperative that we choose examples that we will actually enjoy drinking. That bottle purchased for 8 F a litre in the *hypermarché* may appear extremely good value compared to the price of wine – any wine – purchased at home, but if it proves to be undrinkable it is clearly not such a bargain, especially if you have bought more than a hundred bottles of the stuff!

Conversely, as duty is levied on volume not value, better savings are available on wines in the inexpensive to moderate range. In France, wines which can be picked up for 15–18 F would cost around £3 in Britain, a discount of about a third. Potential savings decrease, on the other hand, as the value of the wine increases because a lower proportion of the price is made up by excise duty. We, therefore, suggest that generally the best ratio of savings to quality can be found in table wines priced somewhere between 15 F and 50 F.

As a major wine-drinking and wine-producing nation, France offers scores of good opportunities to purchase wines of all levels. In a country where wine is still considered as something of an essential element of every meal, it is not surprising that much is purchased in supermarkets and *hypermarchés* along with the salt and pepper. *Epiceries fines* – specialist grocers – also offer good, personal selections of wine alongside other gourmet foodstuffs. There are some excellent wine warehouse operations, as well as scores of new, in some cases literally fly-by-night, high-volume cash-and-carrys set up to serve the ever growing number of British crossing over regularly to purchase wines and especially beers.

A further welcome new development has been made by a few enterprising British wine merchants who have already set up branches in France, a trend that is surely set to continue.

Le Vieux Chais, Fressin

Champagne René Geoffroy, Cumières

Meanwhile, in some of the region's finest hotels, guests can purchase from excellent private cellars at reasonable prices. Perhaps best of all, of course, fine growers' Champagnes can be purchased direct at the source, *chez le viticulteur*.

Choosing Wine
The choice of what you actually purchase is, of course, entirely up to you. Taste is, after all, a wholly personal affair. However, it may be worth bearing in mind a couple of general caveats. Firstly, don't consider purchasing quantities of the cheapest plonk available, often indicated on the label as a mixture of wines from various EC countries. Most examples are really little better than the dregs of an already overflowing and bottomless European wine lake. Secondly, it is very difficult to find sound, rock-bottom priced, cheap white wines, so if you prefer white to red then pay a little more for your selection. On the other hand, there is no shortage of sound, characterful and inexpensive country red wines that can give lots of enjoyment and pleasure for half the price of their equivalents available in the UK.

To ensure that you don't end up with duff wines at worst, indifferent wines at best, it is essential that you taste before you buy. While in some outlets this may be possible, certainly in most it is not usually so. To organize a simple tasting for yourself may seem like a lot of trouble but believe us, it is worth it, especially if you are considering bringing home

anything like your full guideline allowances. If there are two of you, for example, that is twenty cases or 240 bottles, which by any standard represents a huge quantity of wine and a not inconsiderable investment of money, so it only makes sense that you know what you are buying. Tasting carefully and considerately is the only way to ensure this (though never, of course, if you are driving). We suggest that you buy a selection of examples from whatever category you are interested in (light dry white, full-bodied red, etc.), and taste comparatively in your hotel room (take along some Vacu-Vin wine stoppers).

On the opposite page are some favourite, good value wines usually available within the target price range. Remember that if there are two versions of the same wine, the more expensive may have undergone a more rigorous selection and care in production. Similarly, wines that have won medals at important wine fairs are generally (but not always) worth paying a little more for. It is, of course, essential to have in mind a good idea of what equivalent wines cost back home. Take with you various wine lists and a current copy of *Websters' Wine Guide* which will help with comparative pricing.

Transporting Wine
Even if you are not intending to bring back your entire permitted allowance of 120 bottles per person, it is still essential that some thought is given to loading and transporting safely large

Light Dry Whites

Bergerac
Bordeaux Sec
Bourgogne Aligoté
Côtes-de-Gascogne
Entre-Deux-Mers
Gros Plant *sur lie*
Haut Poitou
Muscadet *sur lie*
Petit Chablis
Picpoul de Pinet
Pineau de la Loire
Pinot Blanc d'Alsace
Saumur
Sauvignon de Touraine
Sylvaner d'Alsace
Vin de Pays de l'Aude
Vin de Pays Charentais
Vin de Pays de l'Herault
Vin de Pays Sables du Golfe
   du Lion

Medium- to Full-Bodied and/ or Aromatic White Wines

Bourgogne
Chablis
Châteauneuf-du-Pape
Côtes-du-Rhône
Gaillac
Gewürztraminer d'Alsace
Mâcon
Montagny
Muscat d'Alsace
Pinot Gris (Tokay) d'Alsace
Pouilly Fuissé
Pouilly Fumé
Pouilly Vinzelles
Riesling d'Alsace
St-Veran
Sancerre
Savennières

Rosé Wines

Côteaux d'Aix-en-Provence
Côtes-de-Provence
Gris de Gris Vin de Pays
   Sables du Golfe du Lion
Lirac
Tavel

Light Red Wines

Beaujolais
Bergerac
Bourgogne Passe-Tout-Grains
Costières du Gard
Gaillac
Vin de Pays d'Ardèche
Vin de Pays de l'Aude
Vin de Pays de l'Herault

Medium- and Full-Bodied Red Wines

Bandol
Bordeaux
Bourgogne Hautes-Côtes-
   de-Beaune
Bourgogne Hautes-Côtes-
   de-Nuits
Cahors
Canon Fronsac
Collioure
Corbières
Costières de Nîmes
Côteaux d'Aix-en-Provence
Côtes-de-Bourg
Côtes-de-Buzet
Côtes-du-Luberon
Côtes-du-Rhône
Côtes-du-Roussillon
Crozes-Hermitage
Fitou
Gigondas
Haut-Médoc

Lalande-de-Pomerol
Mâcon
Madiran
Médoc
Mercurey
Minervois
Montagne-St-Emilion
Pécharmant
Rully
St-Emilion
Vacqueyras
Vin de Pays Collines
   Rhodaniennes

Sweet Wines and Fortified Sweet Wines

Banyuls
Barsac
Cérons
Côteaux-du-Layon
Loupiac
Monbazillac
Montlouis
Muscat de Beaumes-de-Venise
Muscat de Frontignan
Muscat de Lunel
Muscat de Rivesaltes
Ste-Croix-du-Mont
Sauternes
Vouvray

Sparkling Wines

Blanquette de Limoux
Champagne
Clairette de Die
Crémant d'Alsace
Crémant de Bourgogne
Saumur Mousseux
Vouvray

quantities. Wine is a heavy and bulky item, so you should ascertain how much you can physically fit into your vehicle before you purchase it. As a rough guide, and assuming that no other items are being transported, an average hatchback with seats folded down may take between fifteen and twenty cases of wine, while a large estate car might just squeeze in between thirty and thirty-five cases. However, once passengers are also in the car, it is essential to check that you have not exceeded your vehicle's payload allowance. Not only would this be highly unsafe, it is also illegal.

The following should be taken as a rough guideline to weight. An average twelve-bottle case of still wine weighs approximately 15 kilograms; a case of Champagne or sparkling wine weighs about 20 kilograms due to the heavier bottles used; and a case of twenty-four 33-centilitre bottles of beer weighs about 13 kilograms. Twenty cases of still wine, therefore, adds about 300 kilograms of extra weight, or about the equivalent of four average adults.

The easiest way to pack wine in a vehicle is in twelve-bottle, cardboard boxes. However, if you are purchasing wine at *hypermarchés* or supermarkets, there may only be a very small, limited, and often uninteresting range of wines on sale in unmixed, boxed cases. Therefore, if you are planning on buying a lot of wine, you will need to bring with you some sort of storage container so that you do not end up with dozens of loose bottles rattling around in the boot. Individual wine outlets and *épiceries fines* usually have empty boxes on hand with which you can make up mixed cases, so this is one important advantage of buying wine in such places.

Remember, wine, once transported even short distances, must be allowed to rest for a short period before being drunk, preferably in a cool, dark space for at least a fortnight. So on returning home, resist immediate temptation.

Only Here for the Beer

While huge savings can undoubtedly be made on wine purchases in France, great savings can also be made on purchases of beer. The guideline allowance for personal transportation of beer between member states is 110 litres, or over 330 33-centilitre bottles, nearly fourteen 24-bottle cases. Visit virtually any *hypermarché* in the north of France and you are likely to see legions of British visitors taking advantage of this more than generous amount, shopping trolleys literally creaking under the load of cases piled high.

French lagers, primarily brewed in northeast France, are remarkably inexpensive and of a good overall quality, if rather characterless and undistinguishable. Popular brands include Kronenbourg, Mutzig, Kanterbräu, and Fischer. The local brew of Pas de Calais comes from the Brasserie St-Omer. Better still is a beer from the same brewery group known as L'Epi de Facon, a light and stylish, quenchingly refreshing wheat beer. Good beers, too, come from Pelforth, brewed near Lille. For our money, though, we would suggest that if you like lagers it may be better to look north to the excellent (if more expensive) premium examples like Stella Artois and Jupiler of Belgium, and Heineken from the Netherlands.

The Classic Beers of Northern France and Belgium: The Thinking Drinker's Alternative

Of course, Belgium and, to a lesser extent, northern France are areas with great brewing traditions. Certainly no other country on earth matches Belgium in the sheer range and individuality of beers produced. Light, slightly sharp wheat beers contrast with dense, dark and powerful brews made by Trappist monks. There are richly flavoured 'red beers', strong, golden, hoppy 'specials' produced by triple fermentation, and sour beers aged in wooden barrels. Lambic beers ferment spontaneously with mysterious micro-bacteria which exist only in a tiny, limited area of the Pajottenland. To make gueuze, lambics are wood-aged, then blended and bottled whereby they benefit from a secondary fermentation in the bottle, while kreik, a somewhat bizarre cherry beer, is produced by adding huge quantities of fresh, sour cherries to young lambics. There are Belgian beers that are so stingingly bitter and hugely hopped that they seem almost undrinkable to the uninitiated, and there are others which are malty and fruity, their cloying sweetness masking a frighteningly high alcohol content.

In northern France, the old Flemish traditions of artisan brewing on a tiny scale also continue. Our favourite such brewery, Au Baron, is the source of tiny quantities of outstanding, strong, top-fermented ales, most of which are drunk at the source where on weekends the brewer himself grills meats and fish over an

Artisan-brewed beers at Au Baron, Gussignies

indoor fireplace converted from a shiny brewing copper. Elsewhere, we love the strong, hoppy, bottle-conditioned *bière de garde* brewed at Jenlain, near Valenciennes, as well as the rich, deeply flavoured Bière des Trois Monts brewed at St-Sylvestre-Cappel near Cassel. This dark, sweet, caramelly, artisan-brewed beer is full of character, something like a strong, not overly sweet brown ale with a distinctive, rich yet irony finish.

Such artisan-brewed beers of Belgium and northern France, virtually unknown outside their own countries, even in some cases their own locality, are so outstanding that it would indeed be a great shame if we did not take the opportunity presented by the Channel Tunnel and the EC Single Market to gain a closer acquaintance with them.

BELGIAN BEER MENU

Throughout Belgium you never simply order a beer. Rather, you are always offered a beer menu and there may be from twenty to over 300 varieties to choose from. Here is our own personal 'beer menu' of some favourites.

Cantillon gueuze, kriek and framboise

Outstanding, classic lambic beers brewed by spontaneous fermentation in an ancient working museum brewery in the Anderlecht suburb of Brussels. Gueuze is a blend of young and old lambics; kriek is made with the addition of fresh, sour cherries, and framboise with the addition of fresh raspberries. If you are in the capital, a visit to Cantillon is a must.

Chimay Blue
A classic, bottle-conditioned Trappist beer: full-bodied and fruity, powerful and rich.

Duvel
Duvel is a devil, a top-fermented, bottle-conditioned beer that packs an outstanding and flavoursome punch. This is a classic, strong Belgian beer to be savoured and sipped slowly, drunk in quantity at your own peril.

Hoegarden *bière blanche*
A quenching, sharp wheat beer, served cloudy, sometimes with a wedge of lemon. Excellent summer drink.

Lindemann's kriek
From a farmhouse brewery in the Pajottenland, this is the finest example of this unique beer that we know: lovely, deep red colour, cherryade nose, and incredible sharp, sour, quenching palate.

Orval
Bottled in a distinctive, skittle-shaped bottle, Orval is the hoppiest of the five Trappist beers, light amber in colour, brewed as a strong 'trippel'. We love its outstanding, stinging scent and rasping, grippy finish.

Poperinge Hommelbier
More than double the normal amount of hops is utilized to produce this distinctively bitter, bottled beer from the hop gardens of West Flanders.

Rodenbach
Sour, wood-aged beer, sometimes available draught; this is a very quenching summer drink.

Sint-Sixtus
Our favourite Trappist beers, brewed and available only at the Sint-Sixtus abbey at Westvleteren, near Poperinge. Three examples are produced in tiny quantities: Speciale 6° (red-cap), Extra 8° (blue-cap) and Abbot 12° (gold-cap), the last being one of the strongest in the world. It is slightly sweet, incredibly rich and full-bodied yet not at all overly alcoholic in taste.

Cider, Calvados and Pommeau

The apple is to Normandy what the grape is to most of the rest of France. *Cidre* is the everyday drink here, punctuated, of course, by tots of calva, the potent farmhouse-distilled apple brandy. This is taken in the morning with coffee, in the middle of lunch to create space for meals that are incredibly abundant (this custom is known as the *trou normand*), in the evening as a post-prandial *digestif*, or anytime in between. Pommeau is the Norman equivalent of pineau de Charentes or floc de Gascogne, made from freshly pressed apple juice blended with calvados, then aged in wood casks. It is a sweet *apéritif* that is much favoured locally.

Of course, the best of these apple derivatives are mainly produced locally by farmers who grow their own apples themselves, ferment and distill on the farm. Factory-produced, commercial ciders, in contrast to those from farms, for example, may taste pleasant enough but they rarely have the soul, the rasping bite, the body and quenching, bitter-sweet tang of the real thing. It is essential and most enjoyable, therefore, to hunt down farm ciders at the source, not only in Upper Normandy but also in the Avesnois of Pas de Calais and the Thiérache of Picardy.

The best calvados, it is generally agreed, comes from the Pays d'Auge territory of the Calvados *département*, where it is double-distilled, aged in wood, and entitled to its own *appellation d'origine contrôlée*. The Pays d'Auge lies outside the scope of this book, but excellent versions are on sale throughout Upper Normandy. Good examples are also produced in the Pays de Bray area of the Seine-Maritime and in the Pays de Risle area of the Eure *départements*. Here the tradition of farmhouse distilling is very much alive, so it is a fascinating experience to track down producers at the source.

Spirits and Other Alcoholic Beverages

In the past, we have never considered it worth bringing spirits into the UK, especially when you had to pay onerous excise duty. Local firewaters enjoyed on holiday rarely have quite the same savour on returning home. Indeed, our cupboard is overflowing with scores of such bottles which will probably never be re-opened. However, the EC Single Market has undeniably been generous in regard to guideline allowances for spirits, too; 10 litres of duty-paid spirits can now be brought back without liability for British excise duty or VAT. Thus, as distinctive quality products are produced in the areas covered by this book, there is certainly an argument for stocking up or, at least, bringing back a bottle or two.

The most distinctive local spirit is genièvre, so-called Dutch gin, a flavoursome spirit with the pungent nose and pronounced flavour of juniper berries that is truly the taste of Nord-Pas de Calais. We have already mentioned that calvados, particularly aged versions, is certainly worth bringing back, too. Another special Norman liqueur is the famous Bénédictine, produced in Fécamp. In Champagne, meanwhile, marc de Champagne, produced from the residue of skins left after the wine-making process, and fine de la Marne, a distillation of still Champagne aged in oak casks, are both highly regarded locally, while ratafia is the favoured Champenois *apéritif* made from the unfermented juice of Champagne grapes mixed with brandy, then aged in oak casks. Try these local specialities, and if you have a taste for them, purchase bottles to bring home.

Moreover, if you are a spirit drinker, check out the duty-paid prices of familiar brands of cognac, whisky, gin, vodka or other favourite spirits in *hypermarchés* and specialist shops alike. They are likely to be cheaper in some cases even than duty-free prices and are certainly far cheaper than in the UK.

DOUBLE DUTY-FREE ALLOWANCES

Duty-free concessions for intra-EC travellers are set to continue until 30 June 1999. Moreover, si the advent of the EC Single Market, double duty-allowances are possible. That is to say, when you travel out and back, you are allowed to bring bac with you double the duty-free allowances. Duty-f allowances currently stand at:

1 litre of spirits or strong liqueurs more than 22% volume alcohol
or
2 litres of fortified or sparkling wine
or
2 litres of still table wine
plus
2 litres of still table wine

A comprehensive range of duty-free goods is available at each of the Le Shuttle terminals.

FOOD SHOPPING IN NORTHERN FRANCE AND BELGIUM

A Continent of Shopkeepers?

The finest feature of shopping for food in northern France and Belgium is the wealth of small, usually independently owned specialist shops, more often than not run by committed enthusiasts whose lives completely revolve around their work and who approach their daily tasks with real passion. Whether the *boulanger* who starts work at 0400 each morning, preparing a range of crusty, sourdough *pain au levain*, *croissants* and *brioches* baked in a temperamental but initimable *four à bois* (wood-fired oven); the *maître fromager-affineur* who has five separate *caves d'affinage* each at a different temperature and humidity for the perfect ageing and ripening of farmhouse cheeses made from *lait cru* (unpasteurized milk); the *charcutier* performing feats of magic in his daily transformation of fresh pork into a mouth-watering array of *pâtés*, *terrines*, *boudins*, *jambons*, *saucisses*; the *pâtissier* who arranges his colourfully glazed wares – *tartes aux fruits*, *gâteaux*, cream-filled *éclairs*, *biscuits* and *feuilletés* – with as much attention to detail and composition as any visual artist; or the *poissonnier* who inspects and purchases his fish and shellfish daily on the *quai*, arguing demonically over price with the fishermen, then, deal struck, sharing a tot of brandy or calva with them in the seafront bar: even today, in a world increasingly dominated by supermarkets and superstores, such

Madame Penez, Ma Normandie, Wimereux

Fishermen at Audresselles

committed individuals remain the pillars of French and Belgian gastronomic traditions.

Indeed, to visit such shops is to take part, immediately and easily, in a daily celebration of life – of living and eating well – which is wholly unique and different from our own. One essential message of this book is: seek out the genuine, the local or regional, the individually produced. Yes, you may pay a little more but you will almost always be more than rewarded with excellence.

à la Charcuterie

We have no exact translation of the French *charcuterie*. The word comes from *chair cuite* or cooked meat, for the art of the *charcutier* is the preparation and transformation of the pig into any number of delectable products.

Nowhere is the ingenuity of French gastronomy more ably demonstrated than in the variety of prepared and preserved foods produced from that magnificent, humble beast, *le cochon*. Each *charcutier* has his own variations of the classics, produced to recipes that have in many cases been passed down for generations. And virtually every town in France has at least one *charcuterie*, the source not only of ready-to-eat foods such as *pâtés*, *terrines*, *rillettes*, *rillons*, hams, dried sausages, *quiche lorraine*, *saucisse en brioche* but also prepared pork products that require cooking like *andouillettes*, *boudins noirs et blancs*, fresh sausages, *pieds de porc* and much else.

Many *charcutiers* are also *traiteurs* and offer a range of prepared meals (in many cases a selection of *plats du jour* that vary each day of the week) which only need to be heated up once home. These are usually accompanied by an impressive range of freshly prepared, cold salads and vegetable dishes: *carottes rapées*, *celeri mousseline*, *concombres au vinaigrette*, *salade de tomates*, *tabbouleh*, *museau de bœuf en vinaigrette*, stuffed tomatoes, stuffed courgettes, fried vegetable fritters, quail's egg in aspic. Indeed, those who have to prepare meals daily in France are singularly fortunate that such high quality, ready-to-eat foods are so readily available. We in Britain, on the other hand, have only an ever increasing profusion of miserable, pre-cooked foods for microwaving as sorry equivalents – and look how we gobble up even those!

SHOPPING HOURS

In the areas covered in this book, approximate shopping hours are 0800–1230; 1530–1900. Many food shops, even in small villages and towns are open Sunday morning. Most stay shut either Monday morning or even all day Monday. Supermarkets, on the other hand, usually close on Sunday but are open on Monday. Larger outlets sometimes remain open at midday and have late opening hours on certain days of the week.

Food Shopping in Northern France and Belgium

LE PIQUE-NIQUE

The *charcuterie* is the place to come to put together really superior picnics to enjoy on the beach, while touring battlefields, or simply by the side of the road. Items such as *pâté*, *terrines*, *jambon*, *rillettes* and the like are usually sold by weight (100 grams is roughly equal to a quarter of a pound) or by the slice. Specify thin, very thin or thick slices (*des tranches fines*, *extra fines* or *épaisses*). The following are some of the more familiar items which make excellent picnic fare.

Fromage de tête Head cheese or brawn, meat from the pig's head, chopped, cooked and set in jelly. Usually sold by the slice and delicious with pickled gherkins (*cornichons*).

Jambon There are many types of cooked and raw, French and Belgium hams sold in the *charcuterie*. *Jambon de York* is a generic term usually applied to any cooked and ready-to-eat ham. The terms *jambon blanc*, *jambon glacée* and *jambon de Paris* also apply to unsmoked, boned and ready-to-eat hams. *Épaule cuite* or shoulder of ham is considerably cheaper than *jambon* and can be excellent picnic fare, particularly if home-cooked. *Jambon persillé* is a terrine of chunks of ham set in a parsley and shallot aspic, usually sold by the slice. *Jambon d'Ardennes*, the finest ham of Belgium, is dry-cured and usually smoked.

Jambonneau Small, breaded hocks of cured pork knuckle, cooked and ready to eat. You can purchase a quarter or a half of a *jambonneau* if a whole one is too big.

Museau en vinaigrette Cured and cooked ox muzzle, sliced, then marinated in a sharp, vinegar and shallot dressing – actually much better than it sounds!

Pâtés Every *charcuterie* worth its salt will offer probably at least three or four of its own homemade varieties, ranging from a basic, coarse and robustly flavoured *pâté de campagne*, through variations such as *pâté de lapin* (pork and rabbit), *pâté de canard* (duck), *pâté de foie* (predominantly liver), or *pâté de lièvre* (hare). *Pâté de caneton* from Amiens is a great, regional classic: duck surrounded by a forcemeat of chicken liver, bacon and herbs, wrapped in pastry, baked and served cold in slices.

Potjevleesch This classic dish of the Nord consists of pork, chicken, rabbit and veal cooked in large chunks, then allowed to go cold in a sharp, vinegary aspic. It is substantial, knife-and-fork picnic fare.

Rillettes Potted shreds of pork, goose, duck or pheasant, slow-cooked in fat and seasoned simply with salt and pepper: excellent spread on crusty bread.

Saucissons secs Air-dried, salami-like sausages, ready to eat cut into slices.

Charcuterie

à la Fromagerie

'On ne peut pas rassembler à froid un pays qui compte 265 spécialités de fromages,' said General de Gaulle – nobody can bring together a country that has 265 kinds of cheese. Indeed, the variety and different types and styles of French cheese is evidence, if any is needed, not only of a vast and varied land but of a people who are highly creative, ingenious beyond belief when it comes to gastronomic matters and, above all, fiercely individual and loyal, not to some central, national precept, but to their own small locality or region.

There are probably well over 300 French cheeses, not counting all the individual and local variations of the classics. Though, as elsewhere in the world, huge cooperative dairies have grown in recent decades and produce a huge proportion of such cheeses in factory-like conditions, the best remain *fromages fermiers*, farmhouse cheeses made by small, individual cheese producers often with the unpasteurized milk – *lait cru* – from their own herds of cows, sheep or goats.

The French, quite simply, consume vast amounts of cheese every day. The cheese course in a meal is as essential as the first or main courses, and restaurants and homes alike are always proud to offer a good selection, all perfectly ripe and mature, to be enjoyed with salad and a glass of wine,

Sire de Crequy

always before rather than after the dessert course.

While cheese can be purchased at supermarkets, *hypermarchés* and *épiceries*, the finest selections are to be found in specialist cheese shops, *fromageries*. The best are owned and run by *maîtres fromagers* – master cheese specialists who are knowledgeable not only of the art of selecting and storing cheeses but, above all, in the delicate and intuitive process of *affinage*, the ageing of young cheeses to maturity and the precise moment when they are in perfect condition to be consumed and enjoyed.

Regional cheeses which should be sampled include the following.

Boulette d'Avesnes A cheese produced from defective pieces of Maroilles, mashed together with plenty of tarragon and black pepper, formed into a cone, and rolled in paprika: intensely pungent in flavour, definitely something of an acquired taste.

Brie de Meaux The best farmhouse Brie, made exclusively from unpasteurized *lait cru* primarily from dairies in the Ile-de-France bordering Champagne and Picardy.

Brillat Savarin Super-rich, super-fattening, mild-tasting cheese made in Pays de Bray from triple cream.

Camembert *fermier* Though this famous disc-shaped, rind-ripened cheese is now made throughout France, the best still is farm-produced in Normandy from unpasteurized cow's milk, cured for about three weeks, then packed in characteristic wooden boxes. The French often prefer Camembert when it is firm and still slightly chalky; the only way to tell the condition of the cheese is to feel it. Ask a good *fromager* to choose one for you depending on how you like it and when you want to eat it.

Chaource *Pâte fleurie* cheese made in small, disc shapes with a characteristic white, downy rind.

Chimay An outstanding range of Belgian Trappist cheeses to accompany the great Trappist beers of Chimay. Six versions are made. Our favourite is rind-washed in beer.

Dauphin A creamy, supple Maroilles type cheese flavoured with herbs and usually in the shape of a crescent dolphin.

Gris de Lille The strongest of the Maroilles type from the Nord: a square slab with pinky-grey rind washed sometimes in local beer, aged until it is almost unbearably stinky. This cheese is also known as Puant de Lille or Vieux Puant (old stinker), an apt name.

Langres Pungent, tangy cheese from Champagne, produced in a truncated cone shape with characteristic, orange rind.

Livarot Strong, pungent, orange-coloured, rind-washed cheese from Normandy. Smaller version is called Petit Lisieux. Traditionally, farmhouse Livarot is identifiable by the bands of natural reed which bind the circular cheese (factory versions use paper).

Maroilles The great cheese of the north: a classic, rind-washed cheese

that, though pungent in aroma, is considerably less powerful in flavour than other cheeses of this type. Maroilles is produced in the Avesnois-Thiérache near the Belgium border, the best from small farm dairies made with unpasteurized milk. Rich and nutty in flavour, the cheese is made in three sizes: whole Maroilles (700 grams), Maroilles *mignon* (380 grams), and Maroilles *quart* (180 grams).

Mimolette Large, orange ball from Flanders based on Dutch gouda types. Hard, aged version can be interesting.

Mont des Cats Produced in the Trappist abbey near Godewaersvelde close to the Belgium frontier, this is a pressed, abbey cheese that is somewhat rubbery in texture with a nutty, mild flavour.

Neufchâtel Delicate, soft, rind-ripened cheese with a downy bloom from Pays de Bray country of Upper Normandy. Neufchâtel is produced in various different shapes – hearts, squares, rectangles and cylinders. The *briquette*, *carré* and *bonde* each weigh 100 grams, the *double bonde* and *cœur* (the most popular form of all) each weigh 200 grams, and the *gros cœur* weighs 600 grams.

Petit-Suisse Soft, fresh, unsalted curd cheese mixed with cream, often eaten with added sugar and fruit. Sold in markets in paper tubes. This cheese was actually first produced in the Pays de Bray but is now made all over France.

Rollot Outstanding, round, rind-washed cheese from Picardy with a spicy, rich flavour. Heart-shaped version is known as Cœur d'Arras.

Sire de Créquy One of the great,

individual, rind-washed farm cheeses of Pas de Calais made throughout the year entirely from own *lait cru*.

Trappe de Belval Another outstanding Trappist cheese, made by nuns at the abbey of Belval near Hesdin: classic, pressed cheese with a hard crust and a mild, creamy interior.

Vieux Boulogne Outstanding farmhouse cheese exclusive to Philippe Olivier, mild in flavour and rind-washed in local beer.

à la Boulangerie

French bread when it is good is quite simply sublime, the crust slightly burned and crunchy hard, the golden-white interior yeasty, chewy and dense. Made only with high grade bread flour, yeast or starter, water and a little salt, it must be eaten as soon as possible after emerging from the oven (preferably a wood-fired one), so much so that the purchase of bread is a twice-daily activity at least. Few would dare to serve bread from the morning with that evening's *dîner*.

Bread is the staff of French life. When it is really good, we are quite content simply to eat it on its own, or with the simplest of French picnics: a nicely ripe Camembert or a *tranche* of *pâté de campagne*, some fruit or a handful of nuts, and a bottle of young, grapy red *vin de pays*.

The French national taste is still almost overwhelmingly for the standard white *baguette* or *pain*. However, many *boulangeries* are beginning to offer a more interesting range of breads. Additionally, most have the usual French breakfast

viennoiserie, including *croissants*, *pain au chocolat* and *brioche*. The following are some of the most commonly encountered French breads.

Baguette The classic, long, thin loaf which we think of as a 'French stick'. Legally, a *baguette* must weigh 250 grams.

Boule Name for a round loaf.

Ficelle Literally 'string'; a very thin, narrow *baguette*.

Fougasse Twisted, unusually shaped loaf, usually baked until quite crunchy; good for *pique-niques* to break off and eat with the hands.

Pain If you simply ask for *un pain* you will get a loaf that is roughly twice the size of a *baguette*, a broad, large bread ideal for a family.

Pain biologique Bread made with organic whole-wheat flour.

Pain de campagne Rustic country loaf, often – though not always – round, slashed and dusted with flour. The best is made with a mixture of white, whole-wheat and rye flour, and has a dense, chewy interior.

Pain complet Whole-wheat bread, usually softly textured, often disappointing.

Pain au levain *Levain* signifies that the bread has been made with a sourdough starter and has been allowed to benefit from a long, slow rise, contributing to both flavour and texture. This is French bread as it used to be, as it still should be today. Sometimes also indicated as *pain à l'ancienne*.

Pain de mie Rectangular, white sandwich loaf.

Pain aux noix Bread made with walnuts in the dough and crust. Can taste quite outstanding.

Pain aux olives Bread made with olives and olive oil in the dough.

Pain de siègle Rye bread (usually made from a mixture of rye and wheat flours).

Pain de son Bread made with added bran.

à la Pâtisserie-Confiserie-Chocolaterie

There is hardly any sight more enticing, more mouth-watering, more irresistible than a beautiful window display of fresh, homemade *pâtisserie*. Whenever we would pass such a display, our five-year-old son, Guy, would inevitably tug one of us on the arm. 'Time for some research,' he'd say, then peel off into the shop to pick out a favourite *tarte*, *éclair* or two. Indeed, it is not hard to keep children well satisfied in France or Belgium

when such simple and pleasing treats are so readily at hand. Some favourite *pâtisseries* and *viennoiseries* include the following.

Brioche Sweet, yeasty breakfast bread.

Croissant The best are extremely flaky, feather-light in texture, yet sinfully rich in butter.

Eclair au chocolat Cream-filled *choux* pastry, topped with chocolate icing.

Gaufre French waffle, best eaten hot simply dusted with sugar. In Nord, these are sometimes sold filled with *crème chantilly*.

Kokeboterom Sweet *brioche* dotted with raisins, a speciality of Dunkerque.

Macaron Almond macaroon, the most famous of which comes from Amiens.

Madeleine The famous classic, delicate, lemon teacakes of Proust's childhood, baked in scallop-shaped moulds.

Pain au chocolat A child's favourite

Temmerman, Gent

at breakfast: buttery, flaky pastry shaped like a sausage roll with a stick of chocolate inside.

Pithivier Large cake or small, individual pastry with a cream and almond filling.

Rabote Apple baked in pastry-like dumpling, speciality of Picardy.

Tarte au citron Lemon tart.

Tarte au gros bord The classic of Nord-Pas de Calais, an exquisitely simple tart filled with little more than a mixture of sugar, eggs and cream. The name comes from the fact that this once homemade staple generally had a thick, hand-formed crust.

Tarte aux mirabelles Fruit tart made with mirabelle plums. The fruit, yellow to amber in colour, is extremely flavoursome, always just a touch tart.

Tarte normande Apple tart made with shortcrust pastry, flavoured with Calvados, and layered with *crème fraîche*.

Tarte tatin Classic, French upside-down apple tart.

The art of the *pâtissier* at times overlaps with that of the *confisier* and the *chocolatier*, so that in many shops, in addition to a superb range of home-baked pastries and *gâteaux*, there may also be a selection of handmade sweets and chocolates. The people of the north seem to have something of a collective sweet tooth, and there is no shortage of regional sweets found throughout. These may certainly be worth seeking out if you have children. Regional sweets, usually packaged most attractively,

also make excellent gifts.

Chocolate, of course, is one of the most famous products of Belgium. Indeed, the Belgians have developed great expertise in the production of filled pralines especially, and virtually every town in the country has scores of chocolate producers and shops. The best are true artisans and manufacture fresh chocolates daily on the premises. Such fresh, handmade chocolates really must be tasted to be believed for they are as different from commercially produced chocolates as can be imagined. They are most

CHOCOLATE GLOSSARY

Praline General term for Belgian-style, filled chocolate (also used in France)

Ganache Smooth chocolate paste made from chocolate, milk and extra cocoa butter. The chocolate may be enhanced with natural flavours such as coffee, fruits or liqueurs.

Gianduja Milk chocolate and hazelnut paste blended while still hot to give a smooth consistency and subtle, nutty flavour.

Praliné Mixture of milk chocolate and finely ground nuts or toffee. The consistency of the mixture can be either soft or firm depending on the amount of chocolate used.

Praliné nougatine The same as praliné only larger pieces of nuts or toffee are utilized, giving a crunchier texture.

remarkable for a subtlety and lightness combined with a chocolate intensity that could be seriously addictive. Fresh, handmade chocolates, it should be noted, are as delicate as any fresh produce. Many varieties of pralines contain fresh cream or *crème fraîche* and they must be handled accordingly, that is, kept at a cool temperature and consumed within weeks if not days. If purchasing chocolates, make sure to have a cool bag in which to transport them, and ask for advice about which chocolates will stay fresh as long as you need them to last.

à la Poissonnerie

Upper Normandy, Picardy, Nord-Pas de Calais and Belgium form a vast, contiguous seaboard. Naturally, in fishing ports large and small, it is possible to buy the freshest catch of the day virtually direct from the boats or at stalls set up alongside the fishing quay. Boulogne-sur-Mer (the number one fishing port in France), Etaples, Dieppe, St-Valery-sur-Somme, Oostende are all sources of the freshest fish and shellfish landed daily and can be enjoyed on the spot at quayside stands – a paper cone of the sweetest *crevettes grises*, a portion of *moules-frites* – or at local fish restaurants. Fish and shellfish can also be purchased to take back home as an inimitable reminder of a short sojourn across the Channel – a tub of *huîtres* packed in damp seaweed or glass jars of *soupe de poissons*.

Given that La Manche is, of course, our own English Channel, and that our boats work the same North Sea as do French and Belgium fishing fleets, it is perhaps surprising to see the much greater variety of fish and shellfish on offer *outre-Manche*. Perhaps one advantage of the coming together of Europe is that we will eventually begin to appreciate more fully that which is literally on our own doorstep when we see that others do. The following glossary may help in selecting both common and unusual types of fish and shellfish from *poissonneries*.

Alose Shad
Anguille Eel
Araignée de mer Spider crab
Bar Sea bass
Barbue Brill
Bigorneau Winkle
Cabaillaud Cod
Coquille St-Jacques Scallop
Craquelot Smoked herring similar to bloater
Crevette grise Brown shrimp
Crevette rose Prawn
Dorade rouge Red bream
Eglefin Haddock
Encornet Squid
Espadon Swordfish
Flétan Halibut
Grondin Grey gurnard
Hareng Herring
Homard Lobster
Huître Oyster
Langouste Crayfish
Langoustine Dublin Bay prawn
Lieu Pollack
Limande Dab
Lotte Monkfish
Macquereau Mackerel
Merlan Whiting

Daily catch

Merlu Hake
Morue Cod (*morue* sometimes can refer to dried or salt cod as well as fresh)
Moule Mussel
Mulet Grey mullet
Oursin Sea urchin
Paling Eel
Paulourde Carpet-shell clam
Plie Plaice
Pouce-pied Gooseneck barnacle
Poulpe Octopus
Praire Clam
Raie Ray or skate
Rameaux des salicornes Samphire, fresh in season or conserved in jars (known also as *passe-pierre* and *haricot de mer*)
Rouget Red mullet

St-Pierre John Dory
Saumon Salmon
Saumonette Dog fish
Seiche Cuttlefish
Sole Dover sole
Sole limande Lemon sole
Thon Tuna
Torteau Crab
Truite de mer Sea trout or salmon trout
Truite Trout
Turbot Turbot

Au Marché
Outdoor street markets, how we love them! Whether we are actually in need of provisions for a picnic, lunch or dinner, or whether we are simply wandering serendipitously, eaves-dropping on local life and colour, we

Shopping for Food and Drink

Brugge market

can never resist a market when we come across one. The very nature of markets – the fact that they may take place just one day a week – often means that it is difficult to plan a visit. Indeed, it may be unnecessary to do so, one town's market being very much like that of the next (even the stallholders may be the same, travelling from town to town on different days of the week). Of course, there are exceptions. Dieppe's great Saturday market, for example, which extends throughout the pedestrian precinct of that important and still charming Norman seaport, is indeed worth a visit in itself.

In countries that are still overwhelmingly rural in nature, markets provide the opportunity for country folk to find a direct, ready and appreciative market for their produce and products. The wizened smallholder in his faded, navy beret who each week brings some bunches of asparagus, a handful of baby turnips and a couple of home-grown lettuce to sell; the attractive goatherd-cum-cheesemaker mysteriously diffident behind her pyramidal piles of *fromage de chèvre* which she has handmade herself; the professorial beekeeper, reading *Le Figaro* behind jars of *miel* and slabs of honeycomb; the *artisan-charcutier*, waxed, handlebar moustache and all, who thrusts out aggressively an armful of shiny *boudins noirs* as you pass by, almost daring you not to buy one: all are part and parcel of daily life in France, an essential experience of being in the country.

We have indicated where possible the market days for some of the towns in the areas covered by this book. However, we stress again that it is often the unimportant, the small, the one-street, weekly markets which can be every bit as enjoyable and provide typical and authentic food and drink shopping experiences. So whenever you happen to encounter one, simply stop and join in the communal, everday fun of it all.

à la Ferme:
Stop to Taste, Stop to Buy

France and Belgium undoubtedly have some of the finest and most enjoyable food and drink shops in the world, many of which are highlighted in this book. Visiting them can be an experience in itself. Equally enjoyable and worthwhile, though, is to track down local and regional products at

La Ferme du Vert, Wierre Effroy

the source, that is, usually at the farm on which they are produced, grown or made. The areas covered in this book offer no shortage of opportunities to do so, and we ardently exhort you to be adventurous and strike out into the country to hunt out fine things to eat and drink. It is far more enjoyable and worthwhile, is it not, to discover your own favourite Champagne grower – *récoltant-manipulant* – who will explain to you how he makes the wines himself and let you sample them in the cool of his chalk *cave*, than it is simply to purchase anonymous examples at the *hypermarché*. It is better, too, to hunt down local cheeses direct at the farmhouse dairies where they have been produced and matured to

perfection, to purchase outstanding, unpasteurized, unlabelled bottles of beer direct from Trappist monks, to seek out the freshest, organically grown vegetables and fruit, and handmade gastronomic delicacies such as *foie gras de canard*, all direct from the source.

We urge you again to be adventurous, to get off the beaten track and out of the towns and cities, to pause wherever you see a sign offering *vente directe*, to stop to taste and buy. We guarantee you will enjoy it, you will have fun, you will encounter outstanding produce and products unavailable in shops, and you will probably make some lasting friends at the same time.

Shopping for Food and Drink

Au Hypermarché

We have exhorted you, above all, to seek out the best independent, usually family-run, specialist food and drink shops. We have urged you to follow dirt tracks direct to the farmhouse source, to be discriminating, to appreciate and discern the best. For in this way we know you will have personal experiences, encounters and gastronomic memories which will remain with you long after the bottles of wine are drunk, the *pâtés* or chocolates consumed.

And yet, we do not deny that the *grandes surfaces* can be useful, even at times enjoyable (though to our way of thinking certainly nowhere near a Channel port). We simply feel that they should not be overly relied on for everything. For all that, *hypermarchés* are undoubtedly the best places to stock up on everyday groceries which are either unavailable in Britain or which cost much more back home. Packaged staples, for example, may not only be better quality, they can also be considerably cheaper. Consider purchasing in bulk such items as stock cubes, dried and bottled soups, tins of lentils and other beans and vegetables, mayonnaise, olive oil, coffee and bottled water. Fresh fruit and vegetables are usually considerably cheaper too, especially that which is seasonal or grown in the locality or region. *Hypermarchés* are also an excellent source of kitchenware, utensils and gadgets not readily available back home. Oyster knives, balloon whisks and Sabatier stainless or carbon steel knives are good buys as are Le Creuset enamalled, cast-iron pots and pans and earthenware terrines and casseroles.

NORD-PAS DE CALAIS

Nord-Pas de Calais, the French region closest to Great Britain, provides excellent opportunities for food and drink shopping. After all, travellers en route elsewhere have, literally for centuries, been pausing here just long enough for final shopping flings and the chance to stock up on those fine French goods – cheeses, wines, *charcuterie*, fish soups and much else – which either did not exist in their own countries or were available here at far cheaper prices. Now that Great Britain is physically linked to the continental mainland by means of the Channel Tunnel, and the EC Single Market is a reality, it is certain that the region is set to benefit even further as more and more of us will continue to come over regularly to shop for food and drink.

While *hypermarchés*, wine warehouses, and fly-by-night cash-and-carrys are undoubtedly reaping the biggest benefits, there are scores of outstanding, typical, small shops – *boulangeries, pâtisseries, charcuteries, poissonneries, épiceries fines* – which should not be overlooked in market towns such as St-Omer, Montreuil-sur-Mer, Hesdin, Cambrai and elsewhere, not to mention in Calais and Boulogne-sur-Mer themselves. Each town has its range of shops which survive not by the trade of a passing army of tourists but through the continual production of fine produce that mainly serves to satisfy the local inhabitants, even if it does cost more than industrially produced equivalents in the *grandes surfaces*. Discovering such shops for yourself is one of the most satisfying aspects of shopping for food and drink in the region.

While clearly there is no shortage of such food and drink shopping opportunities in Nord-Pas de Calais, what is far less well known is that the region is the outstanding source of a range of excellent farm-made and artisan-made produce and products. Indeed, we urge the curious gastronomic traveller to get out of the large and obvious shopping centres, and track down regional and local specialities at the source – artisan-brewed beers, farmhouse cheeses,

Ramparts, Montreuil-sur-Mer

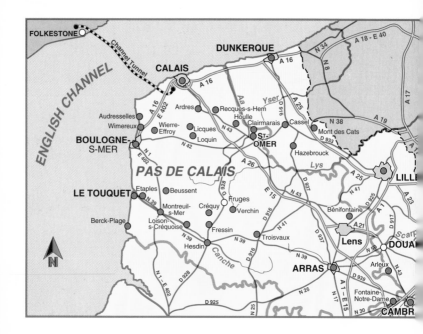

smoked garlic, fruits, cider, free-range poultry, *foie gras*, *soupe de poissons*, handmade sweets and chocolates, and much else besides. There is considerable scope here for the adventurous gourmet to discover many new areas and fine gastronomic delights to eat and drink.

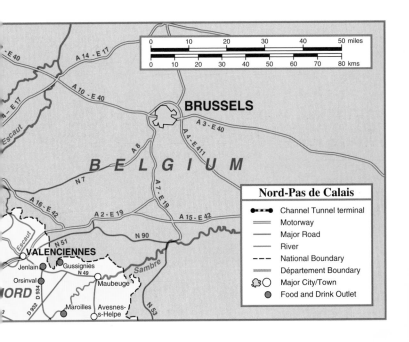

DON'T MISS ...

soupe de poissons (Le Touquet)

smoked garlic (Arleux)

local beers (Jenlain, Gussignies, Bénifontaine)

Philippe Olivier's cheese shops (Boulogne, Lille)

wine buying opportunities (Boulogne, Calais, Ardres, Hesdin and elsewhere)

andouillettes (Cambrai and Arras)

bêtises de Cambrai (Cambrai)

handmade chocolates (Beussent)

handmade lollipops and sweets (Berck-Plage)

62610 ARDRES (PAS DE CALAIS) 🏨
Calais 17 km – Boulogne-sur-Mer 35 km – St-Omer 26 km

CAVE À VINS

Le Chai Ardrésien
681, avenue de Calais
tel.: 21 36 26 26
fax: 21 38 50 75

Paul and Beatrice Jones, an English couple who have lived in France since 1988, have recently opened a conveniently located wine shop en route to Calais. Paul has on offer a number of good wines from throughout France, mainly from small *propriétaires-récoltants* whose wines he has all personally tasted. All except the most expensive can be tasted in the shop before buying. Worth singling out include Château de Trignon Gigondas, Château de Mercuès Cahors, Château Bel-Air Monbazillac, gold-medal Alsace wines from the Domaine Viticole de Colmar, and good growers' Muscadet, Gros Plant and Minervois. This is a wine outlet that is worth checking out, not least because of its convenient situation and because Paul and Beatrice are so helpful.

No credit cards at present but payment by English cash, personal cheque or Eurocheque

---

59151 ARLEUX (NORD)
Festival   *Fête de l'Ail*   first week of Sept.
Calais 139 km – Arras 27 km – Cambrai 18 km

SMOKED GARLIC

La Petite Ferme
9, rue Fily
tel.: 27 89 50 77

In the midst of a dull, northern landscape, on the flat Flemish plain between Arras and Douai, Arleux comes as something of a welcome surprise, an entire town redolent of

L'ail fumé d'Arleux

the garlic scents of the sun. As you approach Arleux, stalls and stands along the road are piled high with literally mountains of garlic, both fresh and smoked, together with bags of onions and shallots, to sell to visitors from throughout the north of France and Belgium.

The Merlin family are garlic growers and in their ancient, resin-rich smoke-house just off the main street, they smoke their own produce themselves. Great braided strings of Arleux garlic, weighing as much as 6 or 7 kilograms each, are hung for up to a week on tenterhooks above a just smouldering fire of sawdust, reeds and wheat chaff. During this time the strings of garlic take on a ruddy-orange hue and the garlic itself is dried lightly to enable it to be preserved for a year or more. In the process, it gains a delicate, not overly strong, smoked flavour and aroma which is distinctive and outstanding.

This *ail fumé d'Arleux* is, indeed, one of the great but as yet little-known, regional specialities of the Nord. Come here, then, to purchase strings of smoked garlic to take back with you, as much as you can carry since it will last you throughout the year. But lash it to the roof rack if you are travelling by car as the aroma inside a closed vehicle is so overpowering it might make you pass out – an in-car aroma surpassed only by the monstrously stinky, local cheese known as Puant de Lille.

Open daily

62000 ARRAS (PAS DE CALAIS) 🏢
Marché   Thur., Sat., Sun.
Calais 112 km – Amiens 67 km – Lille 51 km

FROMAGERIE

**Jean-Claude
Leclercq,
Artisan Fromager
Affineur**
39, place des Héros
tel.: 21 71 47 85

*Goat's cheese at
Fromagerie
Leclercq, Arras*

During both world wars, the inhabitants of Arras were forced to take refuge underground in the extensive warren of *caves* which snake their way below the streets of this ancient city. Today, Monsieur Jean-Claude Leclercq, *maître fromager*, utilizes the old *caves* below his shop for maturing an outstanding range of French cheeses, including the finest local and regional varieties: Maroilles, Vieux Lille, Le Cœur d'Arras, Boulette d'Avesnes, Dauphin, Tomme de Cambrai (aged in local *bière de garde*), La Trappe de Belval, Mimolette, Boule de Lille (a sort of long-aged Vieille Mimolette type), and a good selection of local goat's cheeses. This is a serious cheese shop which deserves to be visited. If it is not too busy, ask to see the *caves* below the shop.

Closed Sun., Mon.

CHOCOLATERIE

Jean Trogneux
33, rue D. Delansorme
tel.: 21 23 62 82

The famous *chocolatier* family, Jean Trogneux of Amiens (see p. 93), has an outlet here in the centre of Arras offering the usual extensive range of handmade chocolates, delicious *macarons d'Amiens*, and one great speciality unique to Arras, the *cœur d'Arras*, a heart-shaped, bitter chocolate filled with *confit d'orange* (candied orange peel).

Closed Sun., Mon. morning

---

*TRAITEUR-
CHARCUTERIE-
RÔTISSERIE*

**Traiteur-
Charcuterie-
Rôtisserie Soille**
11, rue de la Housse
tel.: 21 71 07 11
fax: 21 71 93 28

Place des Héros, Arras

This fantastic *traiteur* located just off the place des Héros offers an outstanding range of homemade *charcuterie* products – *terrines*, *pâtés*, *jambon braisé* and much else – as well as prepared foods like *quiche lorraine*, *flamiche aux poireaux*, *tarte au Maroilles*, rare roast beef, spit-roasted chickens, cooked pork, and a good range of freshly prepared salads and sandwiches. This is the place to come to put together a substantial picnic to take out with you to the sad battlefields and monuments that surround Arras. We can't say that in visiting such places you will feel much like eating but they need and deserve to be visited by all, nonetheless.

A sister establishment to this *traiteur*, the Boucherie Soille, is located just around the corner on the rue des Balances. It is the best source of the famous *andouillette d'Arras* which is made with pure *fraise de veau*.

Closed Sun., Mon. ❖ Credit cards: Visa/CB, Eurocard/Access

62164 AUDRESSELLES (PAS DE CALAIS)

Calais 28 km – Boulogne-sur-Mer 13 km

VENTE DES MOULES, CRABES, HOMARDS AND POISSONS

Chez Michel
235, rue Edouard Quenu
(bottom road just above the beach)

Audresselles is a small, still wholly unspoiled fishing village on the coast between Calais and Boulogne. In the past, its inhabitants lived almost wholly by fishing and there are still those who take their small, deep, stout fishing boats – *les flobards* – to sea each day, winching them back up the beach at night, then pulling them by tractor to their homes. Audresselles has long been famous for its *moules*, as well as for shellfish like *crabe* and *homard*. Come here, then, to see the fishermen's houses, and to purchase shellfish as well as a selection of the daily catch, direct off the boats.

Open daily

Audresselles

62410 BÉNIFONTAINE (PAS DE CALAIS)
Calais 104 km – Lille 36 km – Arras 27 km

BRASSERIE
ARTISANALE

Brasserie Castelain
13 rue Pasteur
tel.: 21 40 38 38
fax: 21 40 20 66

The Brasserie Castelain is one of the few remaining examples of the artisan breweries which were once found throughout the north of France. The company's flagship, Ch'ti, is a classic *bière de garde*, produced from high quality malt, local hops, and pure water from the brewery's own source. It is bottled unpasteurized in three versions: *blonde*, *ambrée* and *brune*. St Patron benefits from secondary fermentation in the bottle *sur lie*. Jade is a *bière biologique* produced entirely from malted barley and hops cultivated by organic methods and guaranteed by the *Nature & Progrès* organization.

Visitors are welcome at the brewery though a telephone call in advance is appreciated.

Open for visits Mon.–Sat. by appointment. Entrance fee includes *dégustation* and a commemorative glass ❖ English spoken

62600 BERCK-PLAGE (PAS DE CALAIS)
Marché   Wed., Sat.
Calais 71 km – Abbeville 42 km – Le Touquet 16 km

CONFISERIE
ARTISANALE

Le Succès Berckois
56, rue Carnot
tel.: 21 09 61 30

Le Succès Berckois,
Berck-Plage

Berck-Plage, like so many other towns on this coast, was almost completely razed in the last war and the subsequent postwar development certainly leaves something to be desired. Still, it may be worth coming here in the spring to see the beautiful fields of tulips in bloom on the town's outskirts, and, if you have children, to visit this wonderful, old-fashioned sweet shop.

Here Madame Micheline Matifas continues the traditional, hand-production of *berlingots* (sugar sweets) and *sucettes* (lollipops). This is candy as it used to be made, produced simply from boiled sugar with added fruit essences and flavourings. The malleable, cooked sugar smells wonderful, and as it is turned, formed and snipped with scissors, it resembles nothing so much as molten glass. The shop has been in Madame Marifas's family since its foundation in 1922.

Open daily. Group visits by appointment Mon. mornings
❖ Credit card: Visa/CB

62170 BEUSSENT (PAS DE CALAIS)
Calais 58 km – Montreuil-sur-Mer 10 km – Desvres 17 km

CHOCOLATERIE

Chocolaterie de Beussent
66, route de Desvres
tel.: 21 86 17 62
fax: 21 81 85 49

The Vallée de la Course is one of the most beautiful valleys in the Boulonnais hinterland, quiet, peaceful and unspoiled. Here, between Boulogne and Montreuil, brothers Alain and Bruno Derick have installed an artisan *chocolaterie* in the basement of Bruno's house. A visit here is a must for chocoholics, for Bruno and Alain produce chocolates of the highest quality, by artisan methods utilizing the finest ingredients. It is indeed a revelation to taste such fresh chocolates (the maximum age of chocolates in the shop is two to three days) for they are marked, foremost, by an outstanding depth and intensity of flavour which, we imagine, could be seriously addictive! We particularly recommend the slabs of dark, bitter chocolate filled with almonds and pistachios.

Alain lived in California for nearly ten years and he speaks perfect English. Both he and Bruno delight in giving demonstrations to interested visitors, followed, of course, by a *dégustation*. Some of their favourite visitors are the coachloads of English schoolchildren who come here regularly ('very appreciative, very knowledgeable,' says Bruno).

Closed Sun. July–15 Sept. guided visits of the *atelier de chocolat* with demonstrations Mon.–Fri. without appointment at 1430, 1530 (English commentary), 1630 ❖ English spoken

---

62200 BOULOGNE-SUR-MER (PAS DE CALAIS) 🏧

Marché Wed., Sat.
Calais 34 km – Le Touquet 32 km

FROMAGERIE

Philippe Olivier
43–45, rue Thiers
tel.: 21 31 94 74
fax: 21 30 76 57

Cave d'affinage,
Philippe Olivier

Philippe Olivier is (sorry) the big cheese, or as the French say, *le gros légume*. This young, dynamic *maître fromager* is, quite simply, passionate about cheese and consequently his small, beautiful shop in the heart of Boulogne-sur-Mer has become famous throughout the world.

Today, in addition to the thousands of French and English customers who come here to purchase cheese, Philippe supplies not only the best local restaurants but also many top restaurants in London and elsewhere in England, making weekly deliveries of a range of excellent farmhouse cheeses almost exclusively produced from *lait cru*. Weekly deliveries of cheeses are dispatched to every European country. Even now, he is sending cheeses to Japan.

Phillipe is a *fromager-affineur*. This means that he purchases farmhouse cheeses direct from a range of individual producers when the cheeses are immature and not yet ready to eat. Then, in his *caves d'affinage* below the shop, he and his team carefully tend the cheeses until they are brought to perfect maturity and perfect condition. There are, for example, six different families of French cheese: *pâte fleurie* cheeses like Camembert, Brie and Neufchâtel; *pâte lavée* or rind-washed cheeses like the pungent Maroilles, Livarot or Epoisses; *pâte cuite* cheeses like Gruyère; *pâte pressé* cheeses such as the mountain cheeses Cantal and Tome de Savoie; *pâte persillée* or blue cheeses; and *fromages de chèvre* goat's cheeses. Each type requires different treatment, indeed, even storage at different temperatures and humidity. Some cheeses need to be turned and brushed every day or two, others are washed in mixtures of salt water, beer or alcohol.

Philippe Olivier is champion of the cheeses of the north. Local and regional cheeses to look out for include the pungent, rind-washed Maroilles and its derivatives Dauphin, Boulette d'Avesnes and Vieux Lille; unique and individual farmhouse cheeses like Vieux Boulogne – actually conceived by Philippe and made on only one farm to his precise specification; Mimolette from Dunkerque; abbey cheeses washed in local beer from Belval and Mont des Cats; and scores of local goat's cheeses. Philippe has also created some unique and individual cheeses which should be sampled. Our favourite is Camembert au calvados, a farmhouse Camembert in which the rind is carefully trimmed off, the cheese poked with prongs, then macerated in calvados, and finally rolled in fine breadcrumbs.

In addition to cheese, there is a selection of different unpasteurized butters sliced from the slab (sweet, semi-salted and salted), as well as *crème fraîche au lait cru, fromage blanc* and yoghurt.

Closed Sun., Mon. ❖ Credit cards: Visa/CB, Eurocard/Access, American Express ❖ English spoken

---

CHARCUTERIE

Charcuterie J. Bourgeois
1, Grande Rue
tel.: 21 31 53 57

Charcuterie J. Bourgeois (formerly C. Derrien) is probably Boulogne's best *charcuterie* and the source of a truly exceptional range of freshly prepared, homemade pork products: *boudin noir, andouillettes, jambonneaux, petit salé, terrines, pâtés, rillettes de canard, potjevleesch,* cured dry *saucisson sec,* and delicious, fresh sausages such as the superlative and juicy *saucisses de Toulouse,* all made on the premises. This is the best stop for provisioning for a superior *pique-nique* (after having already picked up your cheese *chez* Olivier). Those who are self-catering or about to take Le Shuttle home should consider the superlative display of freshly prepared *plats cuisinés* on offer. How we wish we had places like this at home! It is Tuesday, for example, and we can choose from a menu of *endives au jambon, poivrons farcis, jambon braisé, poulet rôti*, accompanied by *gratiné de courgettes*. For dessert, a delicious, flaky *feuilleté aux pommes*.

Closed Sun. afternoon, Mon.

Potjevleesch

BOULANGERIE-PÂTISSERIE

Tout au Beurre
44–46, rue de Lille
tel.: 21 80 50 52

Boulogne's *haute-ville*, or upper town, is infinitely more atmospheric than the duller, more utilitarian *basse-ville* down below but it is generally dismissed as something of a desert for those in search of good things to eat or drink. This outstanding bread shop, then, is something of a find. Here the Joly-Desenclos family bake in a wood-fired oven the most varied and outstanding range of rural and regional breads we have yet discovered. This is bread made the old, time-honoured way, using a *levain* sourdough starter and with no recourse to preservatives of any kind. Nonetheless, these old-fashioned breads will last for up to ten days, in contrast to the modern airy *baguettes* which often seem to go stale literally within a few hours. Some of the breads regularly on offer include *pain complet aux noix, pain complet aux raisins, pain de campagne, pain méridional, pain au levain, pain campagnard, fougasse, pain de soja, pain diététique* and much else.

Closed Mon.

PÂTISSERIE-CONFISERIE-SALON DE THÉ

Au Cornet d'Amour
91, rue Thiers
tel.: 21 31 65 89

This centrally located and popular Boulogne shop offers a highly acclaimed range of *pâtisseries*, homemade ice creams and chocolates. The full range of products can be sampled in the adjoining *salon de thé*. This is a good place to stop for a break and a cup coffee during or after shopping.

Closed Sun. ❖ Credit cards: Visa/CB, Eurocard/Access ❖ English spoken

---

FRUITS SECS

Idriss
24, Grande Rue
tel.: 21 30 54 59

The overwhelming aroma of exotic fruits and spices greets you as you enter this small shop just up from the Eglise St-Nicolas, and on a rainy, grey, northern day, it suggests far-off lands and far-away places. Driss Samouh came to Boulogne as a young child when his parents emigrated from Morocco in 1966. They themselves had been merchants, so in a sense he was following family tradition when he opened this unique shop in 1982. The locals come here, above all, to purchase *pruneaux d'Agen* and Malaga raisins for their tarts and pastries for they appreciate that he keeps only the best quality. But there is much else too: *fruits confits* from Provence, a range of *loukoums* (Turkish delight), dried pears, peaches, apricots, bananas, apples, kumquats, pineapples, papaya and much else.

Closed Mon. ❖ Credit cards: Visa/CB, Eurocard/Access ❖ English spoken

---

FOIE GRAS AND OTHER PRODUITS FROM SOUTHWEST FRANCE

Comtesse du Barry
35, Grande Rue
tel.: 21 87 19 20

Madame Cécile Danvin, the charming, young owner of this high-quality delicatessan, has many English customers who come here regularly to buy the superb Comtesse du Barry *foie gras de canard*. Accordingly, she is happy to advise on this great culinary delicacy and she stocks a full range of different types and qualities. The finest, with a pronounced yet delicate flavour, is whole *foie gras mi-cuit* packaged *sous-vide* in a vacuum bag. But this is also the most delicate and needs to be kept refrigerated during transport. Some customers, therefore, bring a cooler bag with them and Madame Danvin can supply ice packs if necessary.

Other specialities of the southwest include a range of *pâtés* and *terrines*, as well as attractive tins of prepared *plats cuisinés* such as *cassoulet, garbure, coq au vin de Madiran, canard*

47

aux cèpes. As *foie gras* in France is usually accompanied by an unctuous, sweet wine, there is also a small but select choice of Sauternes and Barsacs, as well as less well known wines from the southwest like Madiran, Jurançon and Pacherenc

du Vic-Bilh (an unusual, delightful, sweet wine that is lighter than Sauternes and an excellent accompaniment to *foie gras*).

All of the Comtesse du Barrry products are attractively presented and make excellent gifts that are easy to transport.

Closed Sun., Mon. morning ❖ Credit cards: Visa/CB, Eurocard/Access ❖ English spoken

Comtesse du Barry, Boulogne-sur-Mer

POISSONNERIE-
TRAITEUR

**Aux Pêcheurs
d'Etaples**
31, Grande Rue
tel.: 21 30 29 28

Just opposite the Eglise St-Nicolas and Boulogne's principal place Dalton, the fishermen's cooperative of Etaples has opened a rather grand and spacious restaurant-*poissonnerie* which serves as something of a showcase for

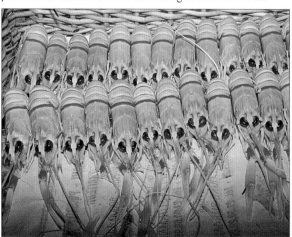

Langoustines

their superlative efforts. Indeed, the extensive display of both fish and shellfish in front of the restaurant is probably the best in town, quayside fish market notwithstanding. On any day, there are likely to be iced banks glistening with an outstanding range of fresh fish, and always a good selection of *huîtres*, *moules* and a tank for live lobsters. Bring a cool box and ask for some ice if you are heading back to England and your fishy feast should arrive home in tip-top condition.

Credit cards: Visa/CB, Eurocard/Access, American Express, Diners

---

CAVE À VINS

Le Chais
49, rue des Deux Ponts
tel.: 21 31 65 42
fax: 21 92 64 80

Le Chais is the closest equivalent to a 'wine warehouse' that we have found, a sort of wholesale emporium primarily specializing in the sale of wines and beers by the case to individual customers. Monsieur Guy Lengaigne stocks over 200,000 bottles of almost exclusively French wines in his establishment located near the train station, from classic wine regions such as Bordeaux, Burgundy, Beaujolais, Côtes du Rhône, Loire, Alsace and Champagne, as well as from scores of lesser known *vins de pays* areas. The business itself actually dates back to 1797, and Monsieur Lengaigne's father, who is ninety-four years old, still works in the office.

Some of the better known and reliable buys include Burgundies from Louis Jadot, Rhônes from Jaboulet and Chapoutier, Loire from Bouvet. However, some of the more interesting and keenly priced wines are from individual growers whose names are little known internationally since many of them do not export their wines. Ask the friendly and knowledgeable manager, Vincent Theret, for advice. He speaks a little English but says in any case that wine is *'la langue internationale, n'est-ce pas?'*.

There are currently lots of inexpensive wines within the 15–30 F price range and every month there are usually about a dozen wines *en promotion*, which usually works on the basis that if you buy six bottles an additional bottle is offered free. There is always a good range of wines open and available for tasting.

Closed Mon. ❖ Credit cards: Visa/CB, Eurocard/Access ❖ Some English spoken

BRITISH WINE MERCHANT

The Grape Shop
85–87, rue Victor Hugo
tel.: 21 33 92 30
fax: 21 33 92 31

Full marks for initiative. Following the completion of the EC Single Market on 1 January 1993 Martin Brown, who owns and runs The Grape Shop in Battersea, was the first to open a British-owned outlet in Boulogne to take advantage of the new, relaxed regulations relating to wine buying and the subsequent invasion of Brits in search of substantial savings. Most, admittedly, still head straight for the *hypermarchés* or cash-and-carrys in search of beer by the car load and the cheapest plonk available. But more and more are finding there way to this serious alternative not far from the Boulogne port.

The biggest thing in its favour is that, for British shoppers, The Grape Shop offers a range of familiar, reliable, and in some cases top-quality, wines at substantial savings over the same bottles sold in Britain. Indeed, the price savings can easily be worked out as the staff will tell you how much the same wines cost in the parent shop in Battersea. Moreover, in addition to French wines, there is a discreet but well-chosen range of wines from Italy, Spain, Australia, Chile, California and elsewhere. Good buys include Rhônes from E. Guigal, Alsace from the Cave d'Obernai, Penfolds and Lindeman from Australia, Chivite wines from Navarra, and a good range of Champagnes and other sparkling wines.

The shop is run by Roger Young assisted by young manageress Katrina Thom. This is a relaxed, friendly and genuinely knowledgable British off-license and there is always a good range of wines available for tasting.

Credit cards: Visa/CB, Eurocard/Access. Payment also by English money or cheque ❖ English spoken

---

HYPERMARCHÉ

Auchan Hypermarket
route Nationale 42
St-Martin-les-Boulogne
tel.: 21 92 06 00
fax: 21 31 24 23

Boulogne's Auchan, located 6 kilometres out of town at St-Martin-les-Boulogne on the road to St-Omer, claims to offer 'the largest choice in the north of France'. It would be hard to dispute this claim for this is indeed an immense emporium, with over 10,000 square metres of floor space, plus a further thirty-five shops, restaurant, bars and a petrol station, all within the same complex.

With over 300 table wines and some forty Champagnes on offer, Auchan has probably the largest wine selection of

all the *hypermarchés* and *supermarchés* in the region.
Bordeaux, in particular, is well represented, with wines in
all price categories including some top clarets and
Sauternes. There is also a sound range of country wines
from the south and southwest: Madiran, Minervois, Fitou,
Côtes de Roussillon, Corbières. Examples from many of the
principal Champagne *grandes marques* are on offer at prices
favourable to those in the UK. There are more than seventy
beers at competitive prices including many of the region's
small production, artisan-made beers. An hourly bus service
runs from Place Dalton to Auchan.

Closed Sun. ❖ Credit cards: Visa, Eurocard/Access. Eurocheques acceptable.
Bureau de change and cash dispenser situated in the arcade

SUPERMARCHÉ

**Supermarché
PG Liane**

Centre Commercial
Liane
boulevard Daunou
tel.: 21 30 43 67
fax: 21 80 90 40

Supermarché PG is a chain of upmarket supermarkets found
primarily in Pas de Calais and Nord (there are some thirty
outlets in total, including four around Boulogne and its
environs, three around Calais, and one at Loon-Plage, near
Dunkerque). PG is probably our favourite chain, mainly for
two reasons: first, because the selection of both wines and
foods is high in quality, and second, because its shops are
usually less overrun with frantic, panicky British shoppers,
madly stocking up on beer since they are smaller and less well
known than the immense *hypermarchés*. Even the smaller PG
branches are generally worth visiting whenever you come
across one. PG Liane, though, located on the way out of
town by the industrial Liane suburb, is the largest and has an
exceptional choice of wines that have received considerable
plaudits for both quality and range. The premium wines are
well displayed in racks. There is a loose-leaf book on hand
in each branch which gives details of every wine stocked,
together with tasting notes and food suggestions.

PG Liane also has a good selection of fresh produce and
products from the surrounding countryside including a
first-class cheese and *charcuterie* counter, fresh fruit and
vegetables, and good home-baked breads.

The PG Liane complex includes some thirty other shops
in the same gallery as well as a café-*brasserie*.

Closed Sun. ❖ Credit cards: Visa/CB, Eurocard/Access. Sterling accepted

62100 CALAIS (PAS DE CALAIS)

Marché   Wed., Sat.
Boulogne-sur-Mer 34 km – Dunkerque 45 km – St-Omer 46 km

FROMAGERIE

La Maison du Fromage
1, rue A. Gerschel
tel.: 21 34 44 72

Located in a corner of the place d'Armes, just by Calais's famous, thirteenth-century watchtower, this is not only the best cheese shop in Calais but one of the most important in the region. Jacques Guislain's shop, which he opened in 1954, may be less well known than Philippe Olivier's famous establishment in Boulogne but, like his counterpart, Guislain is one of the select *maître fromager de la Guilde des Fromagers* of which there are fewer than sixty in the whole country. Thus, in his *caves d'affinage* (not located here but in the centre of Calais), Monsieur Guislain attends to, and oversees, the development to perfect maturation of an important range of cheeses, first from Pas de Calais and the Nord, then from the rest of France and even a few from abroad, too. Naturally, he supplies all the best restaurants in Calais and its environs.

Jacques Guislain is a true artisan and enthusiast. He will take great care to advise you on local cheeses as well as the precise moment a cheese should be ready to enjoy at its best. That is to say, if you ask, he will, through vigorous and expert manipulation with his thumbs, differentiate for you between a Camembert *fermier* that is just ready to eat on a

La Maison du Fromage, Calais

picnic today, and one that would be perfect to crown a dinner party Saturday week. Local cheeses which he singles out as particularly noteworthy include Bergues, Trappe de Belval, Sire de Créquy, Vieux Samer, and any number of local *fromages de chèvre*.

Closed Sun., Mon. morning ❖ English spoken

CHARCUTERIE

Charcuterie René Bellynck
10, rue Royale
tel.: 21 34 49 77

While Monsieur René Bellynck, *chevalier de la charcuterie de France*, is in the back preparing *terrines*, *pâtés*, *rillettes de porc et d'oies*, *petit salé*, *jambonneau* and *jambon*, the charming Madame Bellynck is in the front serving customers, many of whom are locals who come in each day for a delicious *plat cuisiné*, ready-cooked and only needing to be heated up. Monday might be *blanquette de volaille*, Thursday *lapin à la moutarde de cidre* – the aromas permeate the shop and are almost irresistible. Fresh, home-cooked dishes like these put into sad perspective our own chilled, pre-cooked, supermarket meals that have become so popular in recent years.

'*C'est un dommage que tous les anglais vont dans les grandes surfaces,*' she lamented to us. It is indeed a shame that most of us head to the *hypermarchés* instead of to small, specialist shops. Not everyone, we reply, for there are more and more of us, we are certain, who are coming to appreciate

Charcuterie René Bellynck, Calais

individual places like this one, where quality foods are freshly prepared each day with passion and care.

Closed Sun. afternoon, Mon. ❖ Credit card: Visa/CB

CAVE À VINS

Le Bar à Vins
52, place d'Armes
tel.: 21 96 96 31
fax: 21 34 68 22

Just past midnight, 1 January 1993, Luc Gille took his antique van across the channel, well stocked with wine, to mark the official start of Europe's Single Market. Luc is a young enthusiast, a great amateur of wine, from simple but genuine *vins de pays* to exalted *grands crus*. Each of the 300-odd wines that he stocks he has selected and tasted himself. He can, therefore, advise his customers accordingly. Better still, any wine in the shop can be tasted by the glass or bottle at the small, welcoming bar in the back. In a town where new wine and beer outlets are opening literally overnight, Luc's Bar à Vins is an established, serious and welcoming wine shop which deserves a visit.

Closed Wed. ❖ Credit cards: Visa/CB, Eurocard/Access, American Express, Diners. Payment can be made in sterling ❖ English spoken

---

HYPERMARCHÉ

Mammouth
Calais-Ouest
route de Boulogne

The Mammouth is, well, mammoth, an immense superstore that has virtually everything under one roof, from groceries, wines and beers to electrical goods, clothing, sporting goods and toys. This is the closest *hypermarché* to the Channel Tunnel. However, Mammouth will lose this distinction in the spring of 1995 when Cite de l'Europe opens a new outlet on the Calais terminal site. But for the moment, this is the place most British visitors immediately head for. Consequently, there is always a frantic atmosphere in the place with long queues of trolleys loaded high with cases of cheap beer. Indeed, this shop sells more beer than any other retail outlet in France! There are special rooms stocked full of it, as well as a smaller selection of premium local, regional and Belgium beers, and cheap wines by the case. For inexpensive drink, and an extensive range of groceries, Mammouth is the place to come.

Closed Sun. ❖ Credit cards: Visa/CB, Eurocard/Access

59400 CAMBRAI (NORD) 🏧

Marché Daily except Mon.
Calais 150 km – Arras 36 km – Lille 64 km

CHARCUTERIE

**Charcuterie
St-Jacques**
7, rue St-Jacques
tel.: 27 81 29 73

Cambrai, an important Flemish market town in the Nord *département*, is famous gastronomically for two things: *andouillettes de Cambrai* and the minty sweets known as *bêtises de Cambrai*. This shop has been providing the town with the former local speciality for over sixty years. 'Here in Cambrai, we love all types of *charcuterie* and we eat lots and lots of it,' explained the *charcutier*, Monsieur Schryve, who appears more than passingly fond of the products of the pig himself. 'Most famous of all, however, is our wonderful *andouillette de Cambrai* which we make with pure *fraise de veau* seasoned only with salt and pepper.' (*Fraise de veau*, for those not intimate with innards, is a frilly membrane which surrounds a beast's intestines.) This young pork butcher also makes daily on the premises excellent *potjevleesch*, good *pâtés* and *terrines* and, another local favourite, sweet black pudding *boudin noir sucré*.

Closed Sun.

CONFISERIE

Confiserie Afchain
Zone Industrielle
BP 197
tel.: 27 81 25 49
fax: 27 81 20 40

A *bêtise* is something stupid or wrongly done. Legend has it that this local speciality was created in the last century when a young Monsieur Afchain, an apprentice *confiseur* to his parents, continually produced *bons bons* which were not up to scratch. His mother, accordingly, called him a good-for-nothing and screamed that he had made *bêtises*. Well, the wrongly done sweets, naturally, proved to be a big hit, so much so that this family business, founded in 1830, continues to prosper through their production.

Bêtises de Cambrai are on sale throughout the town (even in the Syndicat d'Initiative), so you don't have to come out to the factory to purchase them. However, it is well worth making an appointment for a guided visit to view the ancient copper boilers, the machines that knead the malleable sugar, and the museum of old tins and boxes. Visitors receive a tasting, of course, and there is the chance to purchase the *bêtises* in four different flavours, lemon, orange, raspberry and the original mint.

Guided visits Mon.–Thur. 0800–1400 (advisable to telephone to make an appointment)

CAVE À VINS

Caves Pasteur
6, rue Pasteur
tel.: 27 81 37 75

An excellent wine shop located just off Cambrai's main square, offering not only a good selection of wines and Champagnes at reasonable prices but also a superlative range of regional and Belgian beers. There is also a choice of six wines *en vrac*, as well as port, Muscat and Banyuls drawn from the wooden cask.

Open daily except Sun. in July and Aug. ❖ Credit cards: Visa/CB, Eurocard/Access

---

CONFISERIE

*5 km W. at
Fontaine-Notre-
Dame*

Ets Despinoy
1519, route Nationale
tel.: 27 83 57 57
fax: 27 83 03 73

The people of Cambrai have torn loyalties for their civic sweetie because the *bêtise de Cambrai* is produced by two rival firms, Afchain and Despinoy, each claiming to be the one and only *véritable*. Having critically tasted them both, we must confess our ignorance and state that it all seems to us much ado about nothing. *Confiserie* connoisseurs with better palates than ours (such as our five-year-old son Guy) certainly have strong, personal preferences (actually, he likes both). Despinoy's works is located in a small, rural town outside Cambrai.

Closed Sat., Sun., and Aug.

59670 CASSEL (NORD)
Festival   *Fête du Moulin*   14 July
Calais 67 km – St-Omer 21 km – Dunkerque 29 km

TRADITIONAL
MOULIN À VENT
FOR STONE-GROUND
FLOUR

Moulin de Cassel
tel.: 28 40 52 55

Cassel is a fine, atmospheric hill town built on the Mont de Cassel that rises some 174 metres above the flat Polderland of Flanders. Climb up from the large Grande Place to the summit of the *mont* to enjoy panoramic views across the flat plain to Belgium and the sea, as well as to visit this well-restored, traditional windmill. There were once, apparently, no fewer than twenty-nine on this slope. Today, only one remains. If you are lucky and arrive on a windy day when the *meunier*, young Alain Desmytter, is working, it is fascinating to view the windmill in action, for the entire structure must be rotated to face the wind. The interior of the mill is equally fascinating with its huge, wooden cogs and levers and the immense, granite stones which turn slowly to grind wheat into flour. This excellent flour is offered free to visitors as part of the admission to the mill. Alain also offers for sale bottles of a rich, dark beer brewed especially for the *moulin*, while on Sundays he bakes bread from his own flour. The proceeds go towards helping to defray the running costs and upkeep of this unique monument to Cassel's past.

Open July–Aug. daily 1500–1800; rest of the year Sun. only 1500–1800 or by appointment

Moulin à Vent, Cassel

---

*PRODUITS
DU TERROIR*

**Magasin de
Produits Régionaux**
Grande Place
tel.: 28 40 59 29

This small shop is a good place to stock up on some of the best farm produce and products of Nord-Pas de Calais including local cheeses, regional beers (Trois Monts, Au Baron, Ch'ti, La Choulette) and genièvres, local *pâtés*, *terrines*, *potjevleesch*, bottled *plats cuisinés* like *coq à la bière*, sweets such as *bêtises* and *gaufres* and much else. There are the makings here for an excellent *pique-nique* up by the windmill, as well as good preserved foods to take back home with you.

Closed Mon. out of season

Produits ðu Terroir, Cassel

59140 DUNKERQUE (NORD) 🏛

Marché   Wed., Sat.
Calais 45 km – Oostende 55 km

FROMAGERIE	This centrally located *fromagerie* is probably the best in town, offering an outstanding range of local cheeses
Cremerie	matured in its own *caves* including the distinctive beer-
La Ferme	washed Fromage de Bergues, Maroilles, Dauphin, the
22, rue Poincare	incredibly anti-social Vieux Lille as well as a range of some
tel.: 28 59 22 25	200 cheeses from throughout France.

Closed Sun., Aug. ❖ English, French, Dutch and German spoken

62630 ETAPLES (PAS DE CALAIS) 🏛

Marché   Tue., Fri.
Calais 58 km – Montreuil-sur-Mer 11 km – Boulogne-sur-Mer 27 km

---

POISSONNERIE-
TRAITEUR

**Aux Pêcheurs
d'Etaples**
quai de la Canche
tel.: 21 40 20 39

The *Coopérative maritime étaploise* was founded in 1958 as a professional organization whose primary motive was, and remains, to improve working conditions for fishermen as well as to guarantee a future for their activities. One way it has achieved this is through the creation of *poissonneries*-restaurants which serve as excellent direct outlets and show-cases for the fishermen's efforts. There are now three such establishments. This is the original one. There are similar fish shop-cum-restaurants in Boulogne-sur-Mer and Lille.

This *poissonnerie* is certainly one of the best in the region, located just behind Etaples's fishing *quai*, the boats of the fleet bobbing on the tide. There is always a vast, impressive range of superlative fish and shellfish on display, while there is also a *service traiteur* which sells excellent, prepared seafood dishes to take away and enjoy at home – *crabe farci, paupiettes de poisson, rillettes de saumon, terrine de poisson, paëlla* – accompanied by a small selection of seafood wines.

Closed Mon., *traiteur* closed Sun. ❖ Credit cards: Visa/CB, Eurocard/Access, American Express, Diners

62140 FRESSIN (PAS DE CALAIS)

Calais 74 km – St-Omer 43 km – Hesdin 11 km

CAVE À VINS-
NÉGOCIANT-ÉLEVEUR

Les Caves du Vieux
Chai
13, rue Principale
Tel.: 21 90 61 43
Fax: 21 81 10 00

Paul Glaçon is the third generation of his family to carry on the traditions of wine merchant and *négociant-éleveur* in the small, country village of Fressin. In his *caves* here, he continues to mature both generic and individual estate wines in wooden cask. In addition to generic wines, such as an inexpensive supple varietal Merlot which he ages for six months in wood, Monsieur Glaçon also works with a number of small châteaux in Fronsac, Lussac St-Emilion, Côtes de Bourg, Premières Côtes de Blaye and Bordeaux Supérieur. He visits a number of properties each year and tastes wines from the recent vintage direct from the vat. Then, utilizing second-hand *barriques* which he purchases from *crus classés* châteaux, he has the selected wines filled at their respective properties, aged there for a further period of at least six months before transporting them to Fressin where he oversees their development. He only bottles the wines when he deems that they are ready.

A range of such wines, selected, aged and bottled by Monsieur Glaçon in Fressin, can be tasted before purchase. We particularly recommend Château Le Grand Trié Premières Côtes de Blaye, Château Le Tour des Combes St Emilion Grand Cru, and Domaine de La Martingue Premières Côtes de Bordeaux. Monsieur Glaçon's wines are, on the whole, more interesting than young clarets often encountered in French supermarkets or wine specialists simply because they benefit from greater age in both cask and bottle. For lovers of claret especially, this is a wine outlet that deserves to be visited.

There are also wines from Burgundy, Côtes du Rhône, Alsace, Beaujolais, Loire, an own-label Champagne, and some rare, old armagnacs. Minimum purchase is twelve bottles, though cases can be mixed. There are discounts for quantity and always wines *en promotion*. Wine tastings can be arranged for groups.

Closed Sun. Charge for group visits ❖ Credit cards: Visa/CB, Eurocard/Access
❖ English spoken

Shopping for Food and Drink

62310 FRUGES (PAS DE CALAIS) 📱
Calais 65 km – St-Omer 53 km – Hesdin 20 km

FROMAGERIE
ARTISANALE

7 km S. at Créquy

Sire de Créquy
route de Créquy
tel.: 21 90 60 24
fax: 21 86 27 72

Sire de Créquy, one of the great farmhouse cheeses of
Pas de Calais, is produced on one farm only by Monsieur
and Madame Henguelle-Laigle, who daily transform the
unpasteurized milk from their herd of sixty cows into this
fine, pungent and distinctive rind-washed cheese. Made
throughout the year, it takes about 2.5 litres of milk to make
each cheese (which when finished weighs 280 grams). Some
10 tonnes of cheese is made annually, all by artisan methods.
After the milk has coagulated and the whey has been drained
away, the freshly cut curds are placed in either round or heart-
shaped moulds, left for twenty-four hours to drain further,
then bathed in brine. This encourages the formation of the
distinctive, orange mould that forms on the crust. The cheeses
must then be left in the *cave d'affinage* to mature. They are
brushed twice a week, as well as washed with salt water, and
after about four or five weeks they have developed their full
flavour and distinctive, pungent aroma. The Henguelles also
make and sell yoghurt, butter, *fromage blanc*, *crème fraîche*
and *fromage aux fines herbes*. These and other local *produits du
terroir* are offered for sale in the permanent *halle de vente*.

The best place to sample these excellent products is in
the family's welcoming *ferme auberge* which is open daily
except Monday. Reservations are essential at weekends.

Open for visits and direct sales 0900–2000. Closed Mon. Group visits welcome
by appointment (20–150 persons) ❖ Credit cards: Visa/CB, Eurocard/Access
❖ A little English spoken

FARMHOUSE
BOULANGERIE

5 km S.E. at
Verchin

Ferme Bocquet
25, rue Maranville
tel.: 21 04 43 66

Once upon a time, not all that long ago, most of the farms
of the Haut-Artois had their own wood-fired bread ovens
on the premises for the production of the home staples of
the area: *tarte au fromage*, *pain* and the favourite, ubiquitous
dessert, *tarte à gros bord*. Today, Madame Bocquet continues
this tradition. Utilizing her own wheat, milled into flour at a
nearby artisan *moulin*, she bakes up to thirty loaves at a
single baking and up to thirty cheese or fruit *tartes* at a time
in the old, wood-fired oven.

Tarte à gros bord,
Ferme Bocquet,
Verchin

Come here, then, to purchase a loaf of *pain à l'ancienne* (made to an old, family recipe), together with a jar of homemade *terrine de lapin* (another country staple of the area), a bottle or two of *cidre* produced by Madame Bocquet's father-in-law, and a delicious *tarte à gros bord*. These make the provisions for an excellent *pique-nique*, and visitors are more than welcome to make themselves at home in the garden of this typical, old Haut-Artois farmhouse.

Open daily

59570 GUSSIGNIES (NORD)
Calais 189 km – Valenciennes 28 km – Bavay 7 km

BRASSERIE
ARTISANALE

Brasserie
Au Baron
place des Rocs
tel.: 27 66 88 61

Alain Bailleux and his family claim that their tiny brewery, Au Baron, is the smallest in France. Certainly, it must be the most beautiful, located in an idyllic spot beside the tiny River Hogneau just a few kilometres from the Belgian border. Indeed, this is distinguished brewing territory where, on both sides of the border, artisan traditions remain strong. Bailleux brews three distinctive *bières de garde* – *blonde*, *ambrée* and *brune* – all brewed in tiny batches of only 500 litres at a time. These are highly distinctive and individual products, made without chemicals, unfiltered and unpasteurized, and

*Brasserie Au Baron,
Gussignies*

bottled *sur lie* so that a secondary fermentation takes place in the bottle. Accordingly, they throw a heavy sediment, so care must be taken when you serve them. Come here to taste these outstanding and characterful, regional brews at the source and purchase the beers by the crate or three-bottle pack.

Closed Wed. The brewery is open for visits at weekends when beers can be tasted and purchased together with full meals (*grillades au feu de bois*) in the adjoining Café-Restaurant. In July and Aug., the café is open daily except Wed. after 1500 ❖ Credit card: Visa/CB ❖ English spoken

---

59190 HAZEBROUCK (NORD)
Marché   Mon.
Calais 60 km – Lille 45 km – St-Omer 20 km

---

*PRODUITS DU
TERROIR*

Le Panier Flamand
31, Grande Place
tel.: 28 40 78 04

Located in the main square of this typically Flemish market town, Le Panier Flamand is an outlet for a range of genuine farm products of the Nord and is well worth a visit if you are anywhere in the area. The shop is run by an association of six family *agriculteurs-producteurs*, each of whom delivers its own products and takes turns manning the shop on a rota basis. Madame Minne, the enthusiastic president of the association, for example, has a dairy farm and supplies the shop with fresh *lait cru*, *crème fraîche*, yoghurt, *fromage blanc*, and dairy-related desserts. One farm supplies free-range eggs and chickens, while another supplies apples and other fruits as well as homemade *tartes aux fruits*. Yet another farmer is the source of seasonal, fresh vegetables, and makes and bottles delicious, fresh vegetable soups. The shop also stocks a range of local and regional farmhouse cheeses including Maroilles, Carré du Vinage, Tome de Cambrai, Mimolette,

Le Panier Flamand, Hazebrouck

Mont des Cats, as well as a range of goat's cheeses. There are farm-made conserves and *confitures*, as well as farm-made *charcuterie*, especially delicious *potjevleesch*, *pâté de lapin*, *pâté à l'ancienne*, *foie gras de canard* and bottled *plats cuisinés* such as *poulet à la bière* and *cassoulet*. Local drinks include fruit juices, cider, and local and regional beers. Come here to purchase the ingredients for an exceptional *pique-nique* en route to the lovely nearby Monts des Flandres country or to stock up on preserves and bottled *plats cuisinés* to take home with you to tide you over until your next visit to France.

Closed Sun., mid-Aug. ❖ A little English spoken

62140 HESDIN (PAS DE CALAIS) 🏠

Marché Thur.
Calais 86 km – Montreuil-sur-Mer 25 km – Boulogne-sur-Mer 59 km

CHOCOLATERIE-PÂTISSERIE

Les Pannes de l'Hesdinois
16, place d'Armes
Tel.: 21 86 81 80

In the eighteenth century, Hesdin supported an important roof tile factory which made *pannes* in a shape that at the time was new to the Artois, having curved edges that slotted together to form light, corrugated roofing. Hesdin subsequently became known for its roof tiles throughout the north of France. Today, the only *pannes* produced in town are the delightful chocolate versions found in this traditional *chocolaterie-pâtisserie* on Hesdin's main square. Monsieur Debril's grandparents were *pâtissiers* in Hesdin at the turn of the century, and he himself was born in this traditional house. In addition to the famous *pannes de l'hesdinois*, Monsieur Debril makes good chocolate *tuiles*, *gâteaux* such as the *pavé hesdin*, and an excellent range of tarts and other *pâtisseries*.

Closed Mon.

CHARCUTERIE-TRAITEUR-RÔTISSERIE

Charcuterie Gervois et Fils
7, place d'Armes
tel.: 21 81 16 01

This traditional artisan *charcuterie* has been in the Gervois family for five generations and produces an outstanding range of home-prepared pork products – *pâtés*, *terrines*, *jambon* cured in *hydromel*, *boudins*, *andouillettes*, and much else – as well as good *plats cuisinés*, roast chickens, and a small selection of fresh salads. Everything here is made daily on the premises so this is a good place to stock up for a *pique-nique* at nearby Agincourt.

Closed Mon. ❖ Credit cards: Visa/CB

BOULANGERIE-PÂTISSERIE

Pichon-Leclercq
rue piétonne
24–26, rue Daniel
Lereuil
tel.: 21 86 81 84

Hesdin was the town where many of the Maigret television episodes were shot. This shop is located on a little pedestrian corner by the tiny Canche river. With its old, traditional houses, stone-paved streets and small bridges over the river, it looks like an atmospheric backdrop for the series. Come to this traditional *boulangerie* for a good selection of breads baked on the premises, including a dense, chewy *pain au levain* as well as some good, buttery *viennoiserie* such as *croissants*, *pain au chocolat*, and small individual fruit *tartes*.

Closed Mon.

FRUITS, LÉGUMES AND FROMAGES

Au Cours des Halles
27, rue de St-Omer
tel.: 21 86 84 52

Monsieur and Madame Margollé-Bruyer are a friendly, young couple who own and run this excellent greengrocers. There are always good, local fruit and vegetables here as well as a range of *épicerie fine* products including *soupe de poissons* from Serge Pérard of Le Touquet, conserved vegetables from Jacquelin, *foie gras* from the Périgord, and a small but intelligent selection of wines. Best of all, this shop is an outlet for a discreet but excellent selection of cheeses from Philippe Olivier, delivered in top condition twice a week. If you are not planning on passing through Boulogne, then this shop provides an opportunity to stock up on cheeses before heading home. Two excellent, local cheeses which should not be missed are Vieux Samer and La Trappe de Belval.

Closed Sun. out of season ❖ Credit card: Visa/CB

BRITISH WINE SOCIETY
COLLECTION POINT

**The Wine Society
Collection Point**
c/o Distilleries Rhyssen
rue Fressin
tel.: 21 81 61 70
fax: 21 81 13 21

The Wine Society currently offers its members the exclusive opportunity to purchase about forty-five of its best-selling wines for collection in Hesdin, in an outlet administered by the Distilleries Rhyssen. The published list of wines currently on offer enables members to know precisely how much they are saving by using this service. For example, at the time of writing, the Society's Champagne on the UK list

Wine Society Collection Point, Hesdin

price costs £172.80 per case while the same wine purchased or collected in Hesdin will set you back £148, a saving of £24.80. Similarly, a case of the Society's Claret, which is its best-selling wine, costs £46.20 in Great Britain but only £33 if collected at Hesdin and a six-bottle pack of the Society's Highland Blend whisky, £87 on the UK list price, costs £65 in Hesdin. Considering the amount of wine which can be brought back per individual, it is easy to more than offset the cost of a couple of nights in a nearby hotel, including excellent meals, not to mention the initial £20 fee for life membership of the Wine Society.

The Wine Society's wines are undoubtedly reliable and of a high overall standard. While the majority of wines currrently on offer for collection at Hesdin are the Society's own-label bottlings, the selection is not confined to French. There are wines available from Italy, Australia, California and Spain. The list, we understand, will probably expand in the future as it has proved to be extremely successful. Should there be any problem with the wines once back home, this can be dealt with through the Wine Society's Stevenage headquarters.

The Wine Society outlet is run by the Distilleries Rhyssen which has its own wine shop opposite the Society's own wine store. Rhyssen's own wines are pretty basic and of limited interest. On the other hand, a bottle or two of the company's highly rectified spirits which it distills itself may be worth purchasing if you like steeping fruit in alcohol.

In order to utilize the Wine Society Collection Point in Hesdin, it is necessary to be a member of the Wine Society. At present, it is not possible to apply for membership on the spot in Hesdin. If you are not currently a member but would like to join, details of membership and an application form are available from The Wine Society, Gunnels Wood Road, Stevenage, Hertfordshire SG1 2BG, tel.: (0438) 741177; fax: (0438) 741392.

Closed Sun. ❖ Payment: members may place orders in advance through the Wine Society's offices in Stevenage. Wines chosen in Hesdin must be paid for in French currency (no credit cards, no cheques)

62910 HOULLE (PAS DE CALAIS)
Calais 33 km – St-Omer 9 km

DISTILLERIE

Distillerie Persyn
19, route de Waten
tel.: 21 93 01 71
fax: 21 39 25 36

The Distillerie Persyn has been in operation since 1812, producing genièvre de Houlle, one of the most distinctive and famous alcoholic products of the north, a highly individual spirit produced from fermented local cereals (wheat, malted barley, rye and oats) triple-distilled in Cognac-type discontinuous pot stills, and flavoured lightly with juniper berries. It comes in three qualities. Carte d'Orée is the usual one at 40° alcohol per volume and aged for one year in wood. Carte Noire at 48° is more robustly flavoured and aged for at least two years in wood. Carte Noire Spéciale at 43° is made from a different blend of cereals (more oats) and aged in wooden casks that previously contained Sauternes.

Come to this quiet and typical *audomarois* village to purchase these distinctive products direct at the source, as well as other typical products which utilize genièvre de Houlle as a flavouring such as *terrines au genièvre, potjevleesch au genièvre de Houlle* and *sorbet au genièvre de Houlle*.

Traditionally, genièvre is drunk very chilled in small 'shot glasses', either as an after dinner *digestif* or in the middle of a meal as *le trou flamand*. It is the taste of Flanders.

Open working hours for direct sales. Visits for groups only by appointment (audio-visual presentation only)

9144 JENLAIN (NORD)

Calais 173 km – Valenciennes 12 km

BRASSERIE ARTISANALE

Brasserie Duyck
13, route Nationale
Tel.: 27 49 70 03
Fax: 27 49 74 81

Jenlain, a *bière de garde,* harks back to the family brewing traditions of the Nord when beers were made in winter to be preserved throughout the year. Today, this dark, strong beer, usually bottled in 75-centilitre, Champagne-style bottles with a wired down cork, is one of the most interesting commercial brews available. It is a totally natural beer, top-fermented from roasted malted barley and local hops, bottled unpasteurized so that it continues to condition in the bottle. At 6.5° alcohol per volume, it is a robust beer of great character.

Though the brewery cannot be visited at present, there is an outlet on the premises for direct sales of both beers and beer accessories such as glasses, trays etc.

Closed Sat., Sun.

62850 LICQUES (PAS DE CALAIS)

Marché Mon.

Festival Fête de la Dinde last two Mons. before Christmas

Calais 20 km – Ardres 10 km – St-Omer 20 km

FREE RANGE POULTRY

Licques Volailles
1, rue du Dr Parmentier
Tel.: 21 35 80 03
Fax: 21 35 02 43

Licques has long been famous as a centre for the *élevage de volailles* – the raising of free-range chickens, turkeys, capons and guinea fowl. Indeed, many of the best restaurants of the region pride themselves on the source of their poultry and specify on their menus *poularde* or *volaille de Licques*. The birds, it is claimed, benefit not only from being allowed to run around *en plein air* but also from a select diet of grain and other natural foods. Licques poultry is widely available in supermarkets and speciality butchers throughout the region. However, if you wish to stock up your deepfreeze with superior birds or come over to purchase a *dinde de Licques* for Christmas, it may be worth visiting either the weekly market or the processing centre itself.

Closed Sat. afternoon, Sun.

FOIE GRAS

7 km S.E. at Bas-Loquin

Ferme Auberge des Peupliers
38, rue du Bas-Loquin
tel.: 21 39 63 70

While Licques has been known as a poultry centre for centuries, the raising of ducks for the production of *foie gras de canard* is a relatively recent innovation. At Bas-Loquin on their farm located in the rich Boulonnais countryside, the Dusautoir family specialize in the *élevage* of free-range ducks. The meadows are very green and lush here and it is the diet of rich grass which gives the duck liver its unctuous and rich flavour, says Monsieur Dusautoir. After three months *en plein air*, the ducks undergo seventeen days of force-feeding to enlarge the livers, a process known as *le gavage*.

The *foie gras de canard* produced on the farm is *mi-cuit*, that is, cooked at a lower temperature than commercial, tinned or bottled varieties. It is considered finer and more flavoursome by gourmets, and is rightly prized as one of the great gastronomic specialities of the region. In addition, the

Ferme Auberge des Peupliers, Bas-Loquin

Dusautoirs produce, in true artisan style, a range of other bottled products – *cassoulet*, *pâté de canard*, *rillettes de canard*, *confit de magret*, *cou farci*, *magret en civet* – all of which can be purchased direct at the farm.

Most of the production finds its way on to the tables of the Dusautoir's welcoming and generous *ferme auberge* which is open daily except Mondays.

Credit cards: Visa/CB, Eurocard/Access

59000 LILLE (NORD)

Marché   Daily
Festival   *La Braderie*   first Sun. in Sept.
Calais 112 km – Brussels 116 km – Dunkerque 75 km

CONFISERIE-
CHOCOLATERIE

Jean Trogneux
La Maison des
Baptêmes
57, rue Nationale
Tel.: 20 54 74 42
Fax: 20 54 77 50

It is hard to imagine, considering Lille's industrial sprawl today, that the city was once surrounded by marshlands that were annually transformed into a sea of irises. The flower is in Lille's coat of arms and is known as the Fleur de Lille, commemorated in a famous range of iris-shaped chocolates of the same name, made with *gianduja*, almonds or pistachios. Jean Trogneux's Lille branch is also famous locally for another regional chocolate, Le Noir de Houlle, black chocolate married with the distinctive, local genièvre de Houlle.

Closed Sun., Mon. morning ❖ Credit Cards: Visa, Eurocard/Access ❖ English spoken

---

CHARCUTERIE-
EPICERIE FINE

La Prairie
33, rue du Sec
Arembault
Tel.: 20 57 31 70

This longstanding Lillois institution which has been in Monsieur Baclet's family for generations, is famous, above all, for its freshly prepared *foie gras maison*, whole duck and goose liver, gently prepared *mi-cuit* and sold in *terrines*. This is about as close to fresh *foie gras* as you are likely to get unless you were to purchase raw liver to cook yourself. Indeed, Monsieur Baclet will sell you *foies crus* if you care to try.

The shop is also the source of other local *charcuterie* products; a good selection of cheeses aged in their own cellars and including such local specialities as Vieux Lille, Mimolette and Maroilles; both fresh and roasted, free-range chickens; and a range of other luxury groceries including

La Prairie, Lille

bottled conserves and vegetables from Petrossian, smoked salmon, some freshly prepared salads, and much else. It is an excellent source of a host of good things to eat and drink.

Closed Sun., Mon. morning ❖ Credit card: Visa/CB

FROMAGERIE

**Fromagerie
Philippe Olivier**
3, rue du Curé
St-Etienne
tel.: 20 74 96 99

Our friend Philippe Olivier is nothing if not enterprising. Not content with supplying cheeses to the thousands of English and French who flock to his seaside shop, to hundreds of restaurants throughout Europe whom he supplies weekly, even to customers as far away as Japan, he has now embarked on an ambitious plan of opening a select range of shops in Nord-Pas de Calais as outlets for his superlative range of farmhouse cheeses, carefully aged to maturity in the *caves d'affinage* in Boulogne. Make no mistake, though, Philippe knows his *oignons*. He is a serious and passionate *maître fromager* and any outlet bearing his name has to be similarly serious. This one certainly is, located in the heart of atmospheric Vieux Lille and run by the knowledgeable and charming Madame Brigitte Varlet, herself a member of the prestigious Guilde des Fromagers. Here she keeps an extensive range of Philippe's cheeses, with perhaps just a sprinkling more of those varieties local to the Lillois who must have an affinity for their strong, pungent and assertive flavours: Vieux Lille, Maroilles, Boulette d'Avesnes, Dauphin, Vieille Mimolette and others. Madame Varlet also has an impressive, daily range of home-baked cheese tarts including *tarte Appenzelle*, *tarte au Maroilles*, *tourte auvergnate*, *tartelet au Roquefort*. There are also breads from Lionel Poilâne of Paris and a selection of wines, local beers and ciders.

Closed Sun., Mon. morning ❖ Credit card: Visa/CB

Vieux Lille

POISSONNERIE

L'Huitrière
3, rue des Chats-Bossus
tel.: 20 55 43 41

This *poissonnerie* attached to one of Lille's most famous restaurants located in the atmospheric Vieux Lille district, is probably the best in the city. Certainly, behind its turn of the century, tile-fronted façade, it is the prettiest. This is certainly the place to come for an outstanding range of exceedingly fresh shellfish (including an extensive selection of *huîtres plates et creuses* from various *claires* including Cancale, the Marennes basin, and Belon), a fine range of wet fish from Boulogne-sur-Mer and Brittany, Scotch and Norwegian smoked salmon, as well as a range of *plats cuisinés*, even superlative *foie gras*.

Closed Aug. ❖ Credit cards: Visa/CB, Eurocard/Access

CAVE À VINS

Cave Rohart
66, rue Faidherbe
tel.: 20 06 29 92
fax: 20 15 07 51

This excellent, city-centre wine shop, run by Monsieur Francis Rohart for the last twenty-three years, does not have an overwhelmingly vast selection but the wines on offer, especially many from small *propriétaires-récoltants*, are good quality and keenly priced. Ask to visit the *caves* where the bulk of the stock is matured. There are good wines from all the classic French regions, especially Bordeaux, Burgundy, the Loire and Champagne. Additionally, there is an extensive range of beers including many from Belgium, a good selection of spirits including old vintage calvados and armagnac, and a better than average choice of wines in both half-bottles, magnums and larger bottles. Discounts are always available for purchases of twelve bottles or more 'by negotiation' (in other words, you had better ask otherwise it may not be offered).

Closed Sun., Mon. morning ❖ Credit cards: Visa/CB, Eurocard/Access ❖ English spoken

---

62990 LOISON-SUR-CRÉQUOISE (PAS DE CALAIS) 🏢

Festivals   *Fête de la Groseille*   Sun. after 14 July
　　　　　　Fête du Cidre　　　third weekend in Oct.
Calais 75 km – Le Touquet 30 km – Hesdin 14 km

SPARKLING FRUIT
APÉRITIF,
CIDRE FERMIER,
PLATS CUISINÉS
AND *CONFITURES*

La Maison du Perlé
50, rue Principale
tel.: 21 81 30 85
fax: 21 86 05 80

The enterprising Delobel family welcome some 15,000 visitors to their farm each year to sample the now famous *Le Perlé de Groseille* and *Le Perlé de Framboise*, sparkling fruit wine *apéritifs* made respectively from redcurrants and raspberries. Come here to the farm, located roughly midway between Montreuil and Hesdin in the quiet and lovely Vallée de la Créquoise, to taste and purchase them at the source, on sale with an imaginative range of quality products which make use of the wines including *confitures, terrines, plats cuisinés* (*coquilles St-Jacques au Perlé de Groseille, poulet au Perlé de Groseille*), and fresh chocolates. Additionally, the Delobels make a good, unpasteurized farm *cidre*.

In summer, there is a pleasant, grassy picnic area with a playground for children. Monsieur Delobel has set up a stall in the grounds where he makes *crêpes à la bière*, and offers *crêpes* menus accompanied by either cider or the sparkling fruit wines. There are mountain bikes for rent by the half or full day for excursions through the Vallée de la Créquoise, as well as pony rides for children, while in July and October the Delobels host the *Fête de la Groseille* and the *Fête du Cidre*.

Closed Sun. during Jan. and Feb. Groups welcome ❖ Credit cards: Visa/CB, Eurocard/Access, American Express ❖ English spoken

59550 MAROILLES (NORD) 🏠

Marché Thur.

Festival *Fête de la Flamiche* Sun. before 15 Aug.

Calais 192 km – Cambrai 42 km – Avesnes-sur-Helpe 14 km

FROMAGERIE
ARTISANALE

**Ferme du Verger
Pilote**

1810, route de
Landrecies

tel.: 27 84 71 10

fax: 27 77 77 23

Maroilles is undoubtedly one of the great cheeses of the north of France, one of only two dozen entitled to select *appellation d'origine contrôlée* status. Jean-Pierre Largillière's farm is the only one actually producing this great speciality in the eponymous cheese town itself. It is, of course, the milk from the rich, green, rolling dairy land of the Avesnois which makes the cheese superlative. At the Ferme du Verger Pilote, Jean-Pierre utilizes only that from his own herd of 120 Friesan cows, unpasteurized, of course. The cheeses age in the vaulted *cave d'affinage* for at least three months during which time they must all be carefully and individually brushed with salt water to enable the distinctive orange rind and flavour to develop.

The Ferme du Verger Pilote is also the source of the distinctive and strong Boulette d'Avesnes (a ball- or cone-shaped cheese mixed with tarragon and black pepper and rolled in paprika), Dauphin (dolphin-shaped, also flavoured with tarragon), and Rollot. These cheeses, together with home-baked *flamiche au Maroilles* and other regional products – *escaveche, andouillettes de Cambrai*, genièvre, *cidre, bêtises de Cambrai* – can all be purchased in the farmhouse shop.

Café shop open daily for direct sales of cheese and other regional products. Guided visits to the cheese dairy and ageing caves Sun. and holidays 1600–1800 or by appointment
❖ Credit cards: Visa/CB, Eurocard/ Access

Ferme du Verger Pilote, Maroilles

CAVES D'AFFINAGE-
PRODUITS DU TERROIR

**L'Abbaye de
Maroilles**
28, Grande Rue

Maroilles, like many great French cheeses, was originally produced by the monks of the Abbey of Maroilles. Today, the abbey is no more but this shop is situated in part of its old, vaulted cellars. Young Maroilles cheese is purchased from individual farm producers throughout the region, then placed in these abbey cellars to ripen to maturity while undergoing *affinage* – turning, brushing, washing the cheeses carefully by hand. The finished, mature cheeses are labelled Maroilles de l'Abbaye and they are indeed excellent. But make no mistake: unlike some of the few remaining great abbey cheeses of the north (Belval, Mont des Cats, for example), these are not true abbey cheeses at all. No matter, they are still excellent, so come here to purchase them all the same, together with other local cheeses such as Dauphin, Boulette d'Avesnes and the infamously stinky Gris de Lille as well as a superlative range of other regional products including *andouillettes de Cambrai*, *cidre*, *hydromel*, *bêtises de Cambrai* and an excellent choice of regional and Belgian beers.

Best of all, try the *flamiche au Maroilles* hot from the oven together with a glass of farmhouse *cidre* (this is the real taste of the Avesnois), then purchase the cheese tarts as well as good fruit tarts to take away.

Closed Mon. ❖ Credit cards: Visa/CB, Eurocard/Access

59299 MONT DES CATS (NORD)
Calais 70 km – Lille 38 km – Hazebrouck 15 km

POINTE DE VENTE
DES PRODUITS DE
L'ABBAYE

**Beurre et Fromages
de la Trappe**
Hostellerie de Mont
des Cats
tel.: 28 42 51 44

If Flanders is generally thought of as boring, flat country, then the Monts des Flandres gives the lie to this. Indeed, the country between Cassel and Bailleul extends over a series of lush, rolling hills that at times give way to peaks high enough to enable them to be called *monts*. Mont des Cats, at 168 metres, is the highest elevation in the Nord *département*, a dramatic rise topped by the Trappist Abbaye de Mont des Cats. Come here to enjoy the lovely countryside and to purchase at the source one of the great abbey cheeses of the North.

The monks who make this Trappist cheese, being of the retiring sort, have handed over the concession for the direct

Abbey outlet, Mont des Cats

sale of their famous cheeses to this welcoming *hostellerie* which stands opposite the abbey virtually at the summit of Mont des Cats. This is definitely a place to visit for making up an essentially simple yet sensational *pique-nique*: the famous Mont des Cats cheese, of course; freshly baked *pain de campagne*; sweet, unsalted butter from the abbey; tasty garlic sausage *saucisson à l'ail*; homemade *pâté de campagne*; and exceptional abbey beer, Het Kapittel, brewed across the border in Belgium in the famous brewing town of Watou. For dessert, there are delicious sweet, cream-filled waffles *gaufres à la cassonade*. After visiting the abbey, enjoy this simple feast in the woods near the summit or in the grassy area by the tall radio antenna.

62170 MONTREUIL-SUR-MER (PAS DE CALAIS)

Marché   Sat.
Calais 70 km – Boulogne-sur-Mer 37 km – Abbeville 42 km

CAVE À VINS-
CAVE À FROMAGES

Les Hauts de Montreuil

21–23, rue Pierre Ledent
tel.: 21 81 95 92
fax: 21 86 28 83

The Hauts de Montreuil is the oldest building in Montreuil. Here in the old, vaulted *caves* below the restaurant, Jacques Gantiez has collected an impressive and remarkable cellar of old and fine wines as well as more accessible wines at all price levels. These can be sampled by the glass or bottle in the wine bar and are also offered for sale by the bottle or case to take away. Monsieur Gantiez is a true wine connoisseur and his collection of historic bottles should

*Jacques Gantiez,
Les Hauts de
Montreuil*

certainly be seen (the oldest bottle is a 'Mountain' from Málaga dating from 1780). Collectors and connoisseurs will certainly appreciate his collection of old vintages of rare, classic wines, primarily the great growths of Bordeaux. However, there are many more accessible wines, too, and prices are not bad compared with other quality outlets. Since the wines can all be tasted before purchase in the wine bar this is certainly an outlet to consider for purchasing wine to take back home.

'*Il n'existe pas de bons vins sans bons fromages,*' says Monsieur Gantiez, an enthusiastic and passionate *bon viveur*, who believes that good wines must be accompanied by good cheese. Thus, in an adjoining, vaulted cellar, he has a *cave d'affinage* where he personally ages and cares for cheeses which come primarily from small farm producers in the surrounding areas of Flanders, Artois and Picardy. Local cheeses include Rollot, Sire de Créquy, Boulette d'Avesnes, Dauphin du Nord, Maroilles, Vieux Samer, Pavé aux Algues (made with seaweed) and others. Each week the cheeses must be turned and in some cases brushed carefully with a mixture of water and salt or alcohol to help them to develop and mature. This outstanding range of cheeses can be tasted with the wines in the wine bar as well as purchased to take away.

In addition to fine wines and cheeses, there is also a small selection of other local *produits du terroir* available for sale, including *terrines*, *confitures*, *miel* and local sweets.

Closed Mon., Jan. ❖ Credit cards: Visa/CB, Eurocard/Access ❖ English spoken

CHOCOLATERIE-
CONFISERIE

Gourmandise
8, rue d'Hérambault
tel.: 21 06 14 86

This small, quality sweet shop stocks a range of excellent products including Belgian chocolates by Mondose, other superior sweets and lollipops, fruit liqueurs and, best of all, a range of fine fruit conserves, handmade in Pau, the most exceptional of which contain no added sugar whatsoever. Indeed, it is worth seeking out this shop simply to try the sensational *confiture de framboise sauvage*. Take jars of the delicious preserves back home as well as packets of sweets and boxes of chocolates for gifts.

Closed Mon.

CHARCUTERIE-
TRAITEUR

Boucherie-
Charcuterie
M. Vasseur
15, place du Général
de Gaulle
tel.: 21 81 76 18

Vasseur's is the place to come to make up a really special *pique-nique* to enjoy on a walk around Montreuil's beautiful and still wholly intact ramparts. Monsieur Michel Vasseur has owned and run this shop for thirty years and he is a true artisan *charcutier*, producing daily an outstanding range of very pure, natural and wholly delicious *charcuterie* products on the premises. He shuns the use of phosphates, artificial colourings and flavourings, and uses only the minimum required amounts of salt and other seasonings. 'Our customers appreciate quality products that are homemade and natural,' says Monsieur Vasseur.

Come here to sample superlative *terrine à l'ancienne* (made simply with pork liver, pork fat, eggs, salt and pepper, and nothing else), *pâté de campagne, jambon persillé* (parsleyed ham in the Burgundy style), and the famous, local speciality, *potjevleesch*, a cold, jellied concoction made from veal, chicken, pork and rabbit. Every day, Monsieur Vasseur also makes a range of *plats cuisinés*, a good varied selection of cold salads and *crudités*, and stocks a small range of cheeses from Philippe Olivier as well as some well-chosen wines.

Closed Mon. out of season

Shopping for Food and Drink

BOULANGERIE-PÂTISSERIE

Boulangerie-Pâtisserie Coulon-Cols
5, place Darnétal
tel.: 21 06 06 19

Janie Hall, the exuberant and enthusiastic English owner of the Hôtel de France, insisted that we visit this bakery to try their *croissants*. Janie certainly knows her *oignons*: Coulon's *croissants* rank among the best we have tasted. Shaped by hand, they are enormous, light and flaky and taste richly of farm-fresh *beurre*. We think Coulon's bread is pretty good, too, and certainly worth picking up for that aforementioned *pique-nique sur les remparts*.

PÂTISSERIE-CHOCOLATERIE

Daniel Fourdinier
place Darnétal
tel.: 21 81 92 41

Located on a lovely, little square, this shop sells especially delicious fruit *tartes* (*poires*, *pommes*, *abricots*, *fraises*, *framboises*, *mirabelles*, *cerises*) as well as a delicious, local speciality, the *étaploise*, a brioche-like cake filled with *crème pâtissière* and topped with flaked almonds. Come here also to purchase bread as well as exquisite, small, individual tarts.

Closed Wed.

Pâtisserie Fourdinier, Montreuil-sur-Mer

CAVE À VINS

Vinophilie
2, rue du Grand Sermon
tel.: 21 06 01 54

This superior wine shop located by the citadel offers an intelligent and well-chosen selection of wines from throughout France. Bordeaux and Burgundy are, of course, well represented but there are scores of minor, less well known wines, too, available at reasonable prices. The wines are nicely displayed and there is advice on whether or not they are yet ready to drink. There are always promotions going on, so look out for the tags offering, for example, twelve bottles for the price of eleven. From simple *vins de pays* to *grands crus*, there are some good buys in every price range. There is also an excellent selection of wine accessories: Riedel glasses, unusual crystal decanters, *tastevins*, corkscrews.

Credit cards: Visa/CB, Eurocard/Access

9530 ORSINVAL (NORD)

Calais 175 km – Valenciennes 14 km

FREE-RANGE
PHEASANTS

**La Grange de
Malborough**
route de
Valenciennes
Tel.: 27 49 14 13
Fax: 27 27 61 42

Monsieur and Madame Collery raise free-range pheasants in over 4 hectares of rolling and lush Avenois meadows completely covered with nets. The nets are high enough to allow the pheasants a great deal of liberty so that they can easily fly around and they apparently enjoy hiding in the tall, uncut grass full of wild flowers. It takes six months to raise chicks to adult maturity and in this manner the Collerys have an annual production of some 10,000 birds.

All of the pheasants raised are transformed on the farm into a range of highly distinctive, original products of the highest quality, bottled in sterile, glass jars. Utilizing an old, family recipe from Madame Collery's grandmother, for example, the couple produce *confit de faisan*, as well as other excellent *plats cuisinés* such as *faisan au cidre*, *faisan au Riesling* and *faisan à la hydromel*. These products are certainly worth seeking out, sampling on the spot together with a glass of Gewürztraminer, and purchasing to take home.

Open for visits and direct sales daily. Appointments are appreciated for groups and guided visits ❖ Credit cards: Visa/CB, Eurocard/Access

2890 RECQUES-SUR-HEM (PAS DE CALAIS)

Calais 16 km – Ardres 9 km – St-Omer 18 km

CAVE À VINS

The Wine Shop
Château de Cocove
Tel.: 21 82 68 29
Fax: 21 82 72 59

The Château de Cocove is a 3-star château hôtel, located not far from Ardres, with comfortable and atmospheric rooms and an excellent restaurant. Monsieur Didier Calonne, the owner of the hotel, is a local wine *négociant* and he has created an excellent wine shop in the *caves* of the château open not only to guests but to the passing public as well. It provides an outstanding opportunity for tasting and purchasing wine in a highly civilized and comfortable setting. The wines on offer (also served in the restaurant and the bar) are both excellent and fairly priced – wines that appeal to English tastes at all levels, from *crus classés* clarets to *vins de pays*. Some interesting wines that we

The Wine Shop,
Château de Cocove

sampled recently include the excellent Muscadet Plessis-Brézet, a fragrant but dry Muscat *vins de pays d'Oc*, and a Cabernet/Syrah blend from the Domaine de l'Abbaye Cabardès. These wines currently sell for less than 30 F and there are usually a number of wines *en promotion*. There are, of course, *crus classés* clarets, too, as well as an excellent house Champagne. The Wine Shop at Cocove is indeed a serious outlet, especially considering that you can combine wine buying with a stay in such a pleasant and civilized ambiance.

Closed 24–25 Dec. ❖ Credit cards: Visa/CB, Eurocard/Access, American Express, Diners ❖ English spoken

---

62500 ST-OMER (PAS DE CALAIS)
Marché Wed., Sat.
Calais 46 km – Boulogne-sur-Mer 49 km – Lille 67 km

EPICERIE FINE

Le Terroir
31, rue des Clouteries
tel.: 21 38 26 51

St-Omer is a lovely town to wander around, especially its narrow, pedestrian lanes and streets lined with old, stone, merchants' houses. Come to this excellent, small, specialist shop on one such atmospheric *rue piétonne*, owned and run by young Philippe Ducrocq, for a range of good things: a small but well-kept selection of *fromages fermiers* made from *lait cru*;

fresh vegetables and fruit; oils, vinegars and conserves from Fauchon de Paris; *foie gras*, *pâtés* and *terrines*; coffee and tea; and wines and spirits (some interesting calvados and cognac from small growers). Monsieur Ducrocq is happy to put together gift packages in wicker baskets or wooden boxes to order.

Closed Sun., Mon. morning

e Terroir, St-Omer

**CHOCOLATERIE-
PÂTISSERIE**

**Chocolaterie-
Pâtisserie Y. Cadart**
1, place Foch
Tel.: 21 38 20 41

Madame Cadart is as famous for her imaginative window displays, which she changes every fortnight, as she is for her superlative, handmade chocolates produced on the premises and her excellent range of *pâtisseries*. In late April when we last visited St-Omer, for example, the window of the shop celebrated the arrival of spring with a garden of beautiful, edible flowers planted in small, brown pots, all made out of chocolate.

*Choufleurs,
Clairmarais*

Shopping for Food and Drink

The two specialities of the house are *le chapeau vert* (little green hat made out of chocolate) and *les choufleurs* (sweet marzipan cauliflowers like the famous cauliflowers that come from the surrounding *marais audomarois*).

Closed Mon. morning

PRODUITS DU TERROIR

Produits Régionaux
2, rue de Calais
tel.: 21 88 04 11

This small *boutique* just off the main square is a good source of some of the best produce of the region and products of Nord-Pas de Calais. Come here for local cheeses such as those from the abbeys of Mont des Cats and Belval, Mimolette, Sire de Créquy, goat's cheeses and others; a good selection of *pâtés*, *terrines* and *plats cuisinés* made by artisan methods and sold in bottles; *potjevleesch*; local honeys and *confitures*; a range of the best regional *bières de garde*; cider and apple juice, and much else.

Closed Sun., Mon.

HYPERMARCHÉ

Mammouth
Centre Commercial
Maillebois
route d'Arques
Longuenesse
tel.: 21 98 78 00
fax: 21 98 26 25

This Mammouth complex is probably just about as immense and overwhelming as the one at Calais but it is generally less frantic and panicky. It offers a similarly vast range of goods including an extensive selection of both beers and wines. While there is a good choice of Champagnes on offer, some of the best buys we have found here are the non-Champagne sparklers such as Clairette de Die Tradition, Blanquette de Limoux, Crémant d'Alsace, Saumur and Vouvray. These wines can be of good quality and offer fantastic savings on similar sparkling wines available in the UK.

Closed Sun. ❖ Credit cards: Visa/CB, Eurocard/Access

HYPERMARCHÉ

Hyper Cedico
RN 43
tel.: 21 88 79 00
fax: 21 38 88 00

Cedico is a chain of supermarkets and *hypermarchés* with branches in Aire-sur-la-Lys, Arques, Longuenesse, Eperlecques, Lumbres, Racquinghem, Wizernes and St-Omer. Though this particular branch is considerably smaller than the Mammouth at Longuenesse, many *audomarois* locals prefer to come here for fresh produce, meats, breads and *charcuterie*, all of excellent quality and at the most competitive prices. The Hyper Cedico also offers one of the best selections of premium beers that we have encountered, including regional examples as well as classics from Belgium along with all their respective glasses. For the thinking beer drinker, this branch, located at the entrance to St-Omer from Calais, certainly deserves a visit.

The wine selection, though not massive, is intelligent and well presented and there is a fairly good selection at all prices. There is, furthermore, excellent *charcuterie* and cheeses and a *brasserie*-style restaurant that is not at all bad. English-speaking staff wear a Union Jack on their lapels.

Closed Sun. ❖ Credit cards: Visa/CB, Eurocard/Access

RUITS AND *LÉGUMES*

km N.E. at
Clairmarais

u Producteur
0, route de St-Omer
el.: 21 38 12 24

Monsieur and Madame Brioul once lived in the centre of the *marais audomarois* among the canals, in their small-holding on which they grow vegetables. But when their young family was growing up some twenty-six years ago, they decided to move to the 'mainland' of Clairmarais. Nonetheless, they still are one of the few remaining *maraîchers* and continue to grow endive in winter, cultivated under plastic-covered tunnels, and enormous cauliflowers in summer, the vegetables still transported to Clairmarais by *bacove*, the traditional, flat-bottomed boat paddled or poled along the canals. Come here to purchase such excellent, local produce direct from the grower, along with a selection of other vegetables and fruits, supplemented, when necessary, with produce from further afield.

Bacoves in the marais audomarois

Shopping for Food and Drink

62520 LE TOUQUET (PAS DE CALAIS) 🏛

Marché Thurs., Sat.; Mon. in season
Calais 63 km – Boulogne-sur-Mer 31 km

POISSONNERIE

Serge Pérard
67, rue de Metz
tel.: 21 05 13 33
fax: 21 05 62 32

Serge Pérard has been cooking his famous *soupe de poissons* in immense, ancient cauldrons in front of his customers for over twenty years, and the aroma of this richly pungent, concentrated essence of the sea now permeates the very streets of Le Touquet. A stop here, then, is obligatory. Follow the crowds and purchase bottles and boxed cartons of the *soupe*, together with the necessary accompaniments – freshly fried *croûtons*, grated cheese and, of course, jars of piquant *rouille* – enough to tide you over through the winter, to give you an inimitable and virtually instant taste of France. In addition to the *soupe de poissons*, Serge now also offers a richly concentrated *soupe de crabes* as well as a smooth, luxurious *velouté de homard*.

This is not just an outlet for soup, however, but a busy and excellent *poissonnerie* with a full range of shellfish and fish on offer as well as an exceptional range of fish *plats cuisinés*. Indeed, the well-heeled Parisians who descend here in season and on weekends throughout the year, earning the resort the sobriquet 'Paris-Plage', are constantly in and out of the shop, their cabriolet Mercedes and Porsches left purring outside, as they pop in for great platters of prepared shellfish *à emporter* elaborate, cooked fish specialities, or pots of fresh

Serge Pérard, Le Touquet

fish soup to take back to their apartments and villas to serve to guests and friends. Who wants to cook when you are on holiday, anyway?

Open daily 0800–2300 ❖ No credit cards

AVE À VINS

e Chais
1, rue de Londres
l.: 21 05 59 83

Monsieur Yves Bardol, who speaks perfect English, is the manager of this useful branch of the excellent Le Chais wine warehouse of Boulogne-sur-Mer. Of course, this shop cannot stock the entire range available in Boulogne but this is a serious wine outlet, nonetheless, with an excellent range of classic French wines including about ten always on special offer. However, unlike in Boulogne, there is no opportunity to taste wines before purchasing. 'We found that it didn't work here,' explains Monsieur Bardol. 'Our English customers who tasted were fine: if they liked a wine they would usually purchase it. But we found that the French, in particular the Parisians, would come in, taste a wine, tell us *"c'est bon"* or even perhaps *"c'est très bon"*, then simply walk out without purchasing a thing! So we had to put a stop to it.'

Closed Wed. out of season ❖ Credit cards: Visa/CB, Eurocard/Access. Payment possible in sterling ❖ English spoken

---

2310 TROISVAUX (PAS DE CALAIS)
Calais 85 km – Arras 35 km – St-Pol-sur-Ternoise 5 km

ROMAGERIE
RTISANALE DE
ABBAYE

bbaye de Belval
ue du Monastère
l.: 21 03 11 65
ux: 21 47 18 15

Since its foundation in 1893, the Abbaye de Belval has produced Trappist cheese by traditional, monastic methods. Today, thirty-three Trappist sisters continue to live at the Abbey and produce one of the great abbey cheeses of the north, La Trappe de Belval.

This handmade cheese is sold in the Abbey shop, together with butter, cream and *fromage blanc* which they also make themselves. Furthermore, the shop offers a unique and fascinating selection of artisan produce and products from thirty other monasteries throughout France and Belgium, including *crème de mûres* from the Abbaye d'Aiguebelle, *le pâté périgourdin* from the Trappist Abbaye d'Echourgnac, *le gâteau breton* from the Abbaye de Campénéac, honey produced by the monks of Lévignac, fruit syrups from Notre Dame des Gardes in Anjou, and other such products. Indeed, as monasteries have traditionally safeguarded and passed on artisan traditions over the centuries, this abbey shop is the living source of a part of the great gastronomic heritage of France.

Abbey shop open daily ❖ A little English spoken

62720 WIERRE-EFFROY (PAS DE CALAIS) 🏚

Calais 30 km – Boulogne-sur-Mer 12 km – Marquise 5 km

FROMAGERIE
ARTISANALE

Fromagerie
Ste-Godeleine
Ferme du Vert
tel.: 21 87 67 00
fax: 21 83 22 62

The Ferme du Vert is a farmhouse hotel with an excellent family restaurant run by the Bernard family. While son Thomas is the chef, his brother Antoine is an artisan *fromager*, and here on the premises he daily transforms some 400 litres of *lait cru* from a nearby farm into a fascinating and outstanding range of farmhouse cheeses. These are all served in the restaurant and are also sold to guests and passers-by. They even find their way into the most prestigious *fromagerie* in the north of France, Philippe Olivier of Boulogne. The most distinctive cheese is the pungent but not overly strong, orange, rind-washed

Farmhouse cheeses,
Fromagerie Ste-
Godeleine

L'Archange (similar to the beer-washed Vieux Boulogne which is available exclusively from Philippe Olivier); Patriarche is a Mimolette type; Le Cherubin is a double-cream cheese flavoured with red peppercorns or shallots; and Le Seraphin is an aged cheese flavoured with cumin seeds. Come here to stay on the farm and taste and purchase these outstanding and original cheeses to take away.

Open daily

BOULANGERIE-
PÂTISSERIE

Romain Magnier
rue de Conteville
tel.: 21 83 92 14
fax: 21 33 61 06

Romain Magnier, a young artisan-*boulanger*, specializes in the daily production on a commercial scale of *pain à l'ancienne* made to a traditional recipe and baked in a wood-fired oven. Today, at his small bakery in rural Wierre-Effroy, he bakes no fewer than 1,000 loaves a day which he sells to local customers as well as to the quality supermarket chain PG.

'The secret of good bread,' this young enthusiast explained to us, 'is not just in the cooking but in the recipe itself. We use high quality flour and a *levain* sourdough starter. This requires a slow, three-hour rise and there is no way that you can rush it.' Magnier's bread is quite unlike what we think of as 'French bread'; it has a dark, crusty exterior and a dense, chewy interior with a slightly sour tang. This bread, unlike most commercial French breads, will last for up to a week without going stale.

If you would like to see the oven in action, as well as purchase hot bread straight out of it, come here daily from 1700.

Open daily

Pain à l'ancienne, Romain Magnier

62930 WIMEREUX (PAS DE CALAIS) 🏛
Festival   *Fête de la Moule*   first Sun. in Aug.
Calais 29 km – Boulogne-sur-Mer 5 km

EPICERIE FINE

Le Terroir
16, rue Carnot
tel.: 21 32 41 33

Monsieur Auguste Corteyn, *chevalier du tastevin*, is himself a great lover of wine and a gourmet so his shop is well worth a visit. The selection of wines is not vast but it is intelligent. Monsieur Corteyn has gathered an impressive selection of old vintages of Bordeaux and Burgundy (the French, it seems, enjoy giving bottles of a vintage dating from the year of the recipient's birth as a special present) as well as a good selection of reasonably priced, middle-range wines such as the excellent Château de Seguin Bordeaux Superièur *rouge* and Entre-Deux-Mers *blanc*.

This is not just a wine shop, though, but also a serious delicatessan selling local and regional fare, and there is an excellent selection of *produits du terroir*, including jars of *soupe de poissons* and *soupe de crabes, rameaux de salicorne* (conserved samphire from the salt marshes of the Côte d'Opale), *saucisson sec de pays au genièvre de Houlle, gaufres*, local *terrines, potjevleesch*, and a range of products from Fauchon de Paris including vinegars, oils, and conserves.

In season, there are regular *dégustations* and each Friday evening from mid-July through August, when the rue Carnot is closed to traffic, the Corteyns put out pavement tables and wines can be sampled by the glass or bottle.

Open daily in summer (including Sun. and holidays). Closed Thur. out of season ❖ Credit card: Visa/CB

FROMAGERIE

Ma Normandie
29, rue Carnot
tel.: 21 32 45 71

'Thank goodness for the English!' says Madame Penez, throwing up her arms. 'They are our best customers. Very knowledgeable and very faithful.'

This small, specialist shop on Wimereux's main street specializes not only in local cheeses but also in a discreet and excellently kept range of cheeses of national and international renown: Camembert *fermier*, Brie de Meaux, Cantal, Beaufort, lots of different *fromages de chèvre* including our favourite Crottin de Chavignol and, unusually, whole wheels of the classic cheeses of Switzerland, Gruyère, Emmenthal and Comté.

There is also a small selection of fine wines, particularly Burgundies from Drouhin, Rhônes from Jaboulet, and Champagne Deutz.

Closed Sun. afternoon; Wed. out of season

POISSONNERIE

Poissonnerie Chez Rozo
127–129, route d'Ambleteuse
Tel.: 21 32 48 31

On the road out of town, north towards Ambleteuse, this small *poissonnerie* is the outlet for three families' local exploitation of *moules*. Come here to purchase direct at the source. In summer, in addition to *moules*, there is a selection of fish, live lobsters, crabs, shrimp and other shellfish as well as a delicious, homemade *soupe de poissons* prepared on the premises and sold in jars.

Open daily

CHARCUTERIE

Charcuterie Carnot
129, rue Carnot
Tel.: 21 32 46 44

This is a good place to come to gather the provisions for a *pique-nique* on Wimereux's Digue seafront. Almost everything is made on the premises. There is a particularly good selection of fresh salads, cooked chicken, homemade pizza, delicious *saucisson sec*, *terrines*, *pâtés* and much else. Chez Carnot is also a good source of tasty, fresh sausages and a limited selection of fresh meat.

Closed Mon.

PICARDY

Picardy, the region which lies below Pas de Calais, linking the north of the country with Paris and the Ile-de-France, Normandy and Champagne, consists of three varied *départements*, the Somme, Oise and Aisne. It is a region which has neither a distinct, well-known, regional cuisine nor a profusion of local *spécialités*. Yet within its bounds, from the salt marshes of St-Valery-sur-Somme and Le Crotoy across to the Champagne vineyards of the Aisne, from the game-rich forests of the Thiérache and Compiègne to the plains of the Somme where great tracts of wheat grow on former battle-fields, there is an abundance of good produce and products and an easy generosity which is evident on the tables of homes and restaurants alike.

Amiens

The lover of good food and drink who passes through Picardy – and it remains almost overwhelmingly a region passed through rather than stopped in, surely a great pity given its mix of towns rich in Gothic architecture and its unspoiled countryside – may not immediately be aware of what to look for, so little known is the region from a culinary point of view. Amiens, the great capital of the region, its cathedral the apogee of French Gothic architecture, is surely the place to start. This is certainly one of the great cities of northern France. Yet at the same time it retains a rather intimate, country feel which no doubt comes from the fact that within five minutes of the cathedral lies a remarkable area known as the *hortillonages*, a fertile zone crisscrossed by canals which, since Roman days, has been the city's source of excellent market produce. Amiens itself has local specialities which the curious visitor should on no account miss, most notably its famous *macarons d'Amiens* and an unusual *pâté de canard en croûte*.

The Somme, which flows through the city, is in many ways a unifying artery for the region. This great river, as well as its tributaries and the numerous important canals that traverse the region, waters the flat, fertile plains of Picardy, which support great tracts of cereals and the large-scale cultivation of superlative soft fruits, particularly around Noyon which each year boasts an important *marché de fruits rouges*. The Somme, and its attendant marshes and lakes, is the source of a wealth of excellent freshwater fish, eels and wildfowl, while where this great river enters the sea at St-Valery-sur-Somme and Le Crotoy, there are vast marshlands which serve as grazing lands for *pré-salé* lamb.

Meanwhile, inland in the *département* of the Aisne, below the atmospheric, medieval, hill town of Laon, the flatter countryside leads to the Vallée de la Marne and the manicured vineyards of Champagne. To the north of Laon, on the other hand, lies an area of great and unspoiled, rural beauty, the

Thiérache, source of Maroilles, one of the great cheeses of the north (also produced in Nord-Pas de Calais) as well as of other good farm produce and products including fruit wines, cider and much else.

Baie de la Somme

DON'T MISS ...

soupe de poissons (St-Valery-sur-Somme)

Champagne producers (Château-Thierry, Charly-sur-Marne)

Maroilles cheese

macarons d'Amiens (Amiens)

hortillonages market gardens (Amiens)

produits du terroir (Château de Chantilly)

fruit wines (Le Nouvion-en-Thiérache)

Shopping for Food and Drink

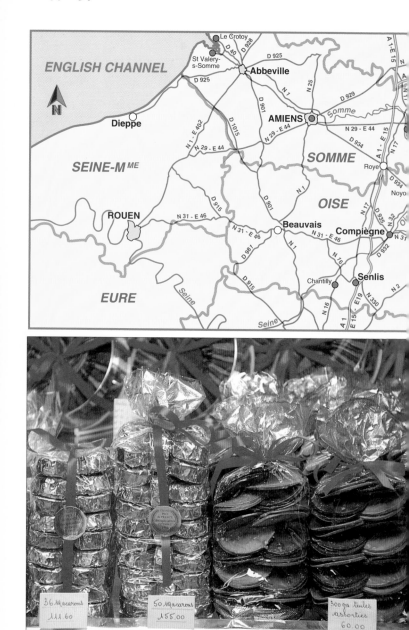

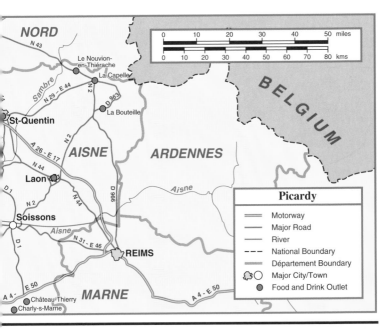

NORD
N 43

Le Nouvion-
en-Thiérache

La Capelle

Sambre
N 29 – E 44
N 2
D 963

La Bouteille

St-Quentin

A 26 – E 17
N 2

AISNE ARDENNES

N 44

Laon

D 1
N 2
D 966

Aisne

Soissons

Aisne
N 31 – E 46

D 1
REIMS

A 4 – E 50

Château-Thierry
Charly-s-Marne

MARNE

A 4 – E 50

BELGIUM

| 0 | 10 | 20 | 30 | 40 | 50 miles |
| 0 | 10 | 20 | 30 | 40 | 50 | 60 | 70 | 80 kms |

Picardy

Motorway
Major Road
River
National Boundary
Département Boundary
Major City/Town
Food and Drink Outlet

0000 AMIENS (SOMME)

Marché Thur., Sat.

Festival Fête des Hortillonages third Sun. in June

Calais 140 km – 100 km Boulogne-sur-Mer – 114 km Rouen

*CHOCOLATERIE-
CONFISERIE*

Jean Trogneux

, rue Delambre

Tel.: 22 91 58 27

Fax: 22 97 96 96

Left:
*Macarons and
uiles d'Amiens,
Jean Trogneux*

On the day we met, Jean-Alexandre Trogneux was ecstatic: only two days earlier, his first child, a son, had been born. The baby is called Jean-Baptiste after the founder of this famous Amiens institution who first bought the shop in 1872 and began the hand-production of fine chocolates. Since that time there have been five generations of the Trogneux family, all named Jean, who have grown up learning the *metier* of *chocolatier* from childhood. Baby Jean-Baptiste, if he follows in the footsteps of his antecedents, will be the sixth.

Jean Trogneux shops are famous throughout the north of France for two things: handmade chocolates and the *macaron d'Amiens*. The latter is indeed one of the great, regional specialities of Picardy, a deliciously simple, chewy, not overly sweet morsel made from no more than almonds

(50%), sugar, egg white and honey, baked until slightly browned then wrapped in gold foil. It is known and loved throughout France and the rest of the world. In 1992, Trogneux's version was awarded the prestigious *Grand Prix de France de la Meilleure Spécialité*, the *confiseurs'* equivalent of an Olympic Gold Medal, at the Salon International de la Confiserie in Paris.

Jean Trogneux is also famous for other Amiénois specialities such as *tuiles d'Amiens* and other handmade chocolates. Indeed, the family's expertise in chocolate making is evident in the model of Amiens's cathedral in the shop window. It took three days to make with some 50 kilograms of chocolate! In addition to the main shop, located in the pedestrian zone of Amiens, there is a 'mini-boutique' at 4 rue Duméril and also an outlet in the Mammouth Gallery. There are more branches in St-Quentin, Lille and Arras.

Closed Sun., Mon. morning ❖ Credit cards: Visa/CB, Eurocard/Access
❖ English spoken

FROMAGERIE

**Fromathèque
Picarde de Gérard
Quentin**
Halles du Beffroi
tel.: 22 92 81 76

The Halles du Beffroi is where the townsfolk themselves shop for their daily requirements, both from the permanent shops in the covered hall open six days a week, and from market stalls that sprawl out over the place des Halles on Thursdays and Saturdays.

Monsieur Gérard Quentin is a *maître fromager* who is passionate about the cheeses of the north and takes great care to ensure that they are aged properly and offered for sale in his shop at the moment they can be best enjoyed. Come here to purchase great, pungent, rind-washed cheeses like Maroilles, Rollot and Vieux Lille from Picardy and Nord-Pas de Calais, and Livarot and Pont l'Evêque from Normandy; the milder local Dauphin and the robust, paprika and tarragon flavoured Boulette d'Avesnes; rind-ripened cheeses made from *lait cru* like Camembert, Neufchâtel and Brie de Meaux; the hard, orange, aged Mimolette from near Dunkerque; abbey cheeses from Belval and Mont des Cats. There is also a good selection of goat's cheeses, butter from the slab, and thick, tangy *crème fraîche*.

Closed Sun. afternoon, Mon.

PÂTISSERIE-TRAITEUR

Le Petit Poucet
12, rue des Trois
Cailloux
Tel.: 22 91 42 32

Young Hubert Fournier is reckoned by many to be the best *pâtissier* in town. The locals come here to purchase *gâteaux* and *tartes* that are virtually works of art, and handmade chocolates and specialities like *macarons d'Amiens* and *tuiles d'Amiens*. Hubert is hugely proud that he is one of the few who still makes a great and famous, local delicacy, *pâté de canard en croûte*, a savoury pie made with layers of *magret de canard* and pork enclosed in a beautiful, hand-raised crust. Time-consuming to make and thus an expensive speciality, this great delicacy should be sampled none the less. Purchase a whole *pâté en croûte*, a nicely glazed *tarte aux fraises* and a bottle of wine, then rent a boat and tour the *hortillonages*, pass the fields of leeks and cauliflowers until you find the perfect spot for a memorable *pique-nique*, the weeping willows, reeds and marsh plants framing the great, ship-like cathedral of Amiens in the background.

Closed Mon.

Hortillonages, Amiens

HYPERMARCHÉ

Mammouth
Route de Paris
Tel.: 22 95 04 27

This extremely vast *centre commercial* is located outside the town centre on the road to Paris. In addition to the inimitable Mammouth, with its usually awesome selection of fresh produce, groceries, wines and beers, there are scores of other shops in the precinct including a branch of Jean Trogneaux (see above). Because Amiens is some way from the channel ports, this immense *hypermarché* is less jam-packed with frantic British in search of cheap beer. Instead, it is jam-packed with just as frantic Amiénois in search of cheap (and good quality) *charcuterie, fromages*, meat, vegetables, fish and household goods.

Closed Sun. ❖ Credit cards: Visa/CB, Eurocard/Access

02140 LA BOUTEILLE (AISNE)
Calais 250 km – Laon 40 km – Vervins 7 km

DEER FARM

La Vallée des Cerfs

Ferme de la Cense
d'Aubenton
Hameau de la Cense
d'Aubenton
tel.: 23 97 49 60
fax: 23 22 10 81

The Vallée des Cerfs is a working deer farm in the lovely Thiérache countryside where some 700 deer are raised annually. There is a pedestrian circuit which takes visitors through the heart of the farm where they can see these magnificent beasts at close quarters. In autumn, the sight of the rutting males in full cry is impressive.

Deer products can be purchased in the adjoining shop and there is a playground for children.

Open for visits July–Aug. daily (except Tue.). Open weekends and holidays only during May, June, Sept., Oct. ❖ English spoken

---

02260 LA CAPELLE (AISNE)
Calais 194 km – Avesnes-sur-Helpe 16 km – Cambrai 56 km

PRODUITS DU TERROIR

Maison de la Thiérache

43, avenue du Général de Gaulle
tel.: 23 97 81 92
fax: 23 97 21 44

The Thiérache lies within Picardy's *département* of the Aisne while the Avesnois is in Pas de Calais; together they form a virtually contiguous area of great, rural beauty and charm. This outlet serves as an excellent source of the finest farm produce from the Avesnois-Thiérache, including Maroilles cheese, goat's cheese, *fromage blanc*, yoghurt, unpasteurized milk, cream and fresh eggs; regional products like *escavèche de la truite*, a delicious concoction of marinated trout conserved in a vinegary jelly to be eaten cold; local drinks such as the Folie Douce fruit wines, *cidre* and local beers; *terrines*, *plats cuisinés* and *foie gras*; fresh, farm produce such as *gâteau au miel*; and much else.

The Maison also serves as an office of information for the region and can provide maps and give touring advice.

Closed Sun. except April–Sept.

)500 CHANTILLY (OISE) 🚋

alais 250 km – Paris 41 km – Compiègne 44 km

?ODUITS DU TERROIR

pécialités du
erroir

 Hameau
rc du Château

There could hardly be a finer, more atmospheric setting than Chantilly's château park for this excellent outlet for superb, regional and local farm produce and products of Picardy. The outlet was conceived, and is run, by the Maison de l'Agriculture de l'Oise and is a true showcase for *les bons produits de la Picardie*. Come here for freshly baked *pain à l'ancienne*, homemade tarts, goat's cheese, fresh farm eggs, yoghurt, honey, jars of *foie gras*, *pâté* and *terrines*, cider and sparkling fruit wines. Clearly, there are the makings here for a superb picnic in the park (be sure to take away all your litter). Alternatively, enjoy these foods at the pleasant tables set up outside for a *goûter champêtre*.

Open June–Sept. 1100–1900 ❖ Credit cards: Visa/CB, Eurocard/Access

hâteau de
hantilly

CHOCOLATERIE

La Tuile d'Or
15, avenue du
Maréchal Joffre
tel.: 44 58 17 77

Chantilly is famous for *crème chantilly* which correctly should be made from unpasteurized, fresh cream. This stylish, quality chocolate shop is the source of two less well known but equally delicious specialities of Chantilly: *bois de cerf*, little 'twigs' of chocolate filled with hazlenut praliné, and *châtaignes*, chocolate 'horse chestnuts' filled with an almond and pistachio paste. Purchase nicely wrapped packets or boxes to take home as gifts or purchase a small bag to indulge yourself.

Closed Mon. ❖ Credit cards: Visa/CB, Eurocard/Access

---

*CHARCUTERIE-
TRAITEUR*

A la Renommée
9, rue de Paris
tel.: 44 57 01 13

While officially, you are not supposed to take food into the park of the château itself, there are still plenty of pleasant, grassy areas between the château and the racecourse where you can spread out a rug and enjoy a range of good, home-prepared foods from this useful *charcuterie-traiteur* including their own *terrines*, *pâté de campagne*, *galantine de volaille*, *hure pistachée*, *pâté en croûte*. Madame Bertheau will make sandwiches for you, and there is a selection of cold drinks, including wine, beer and cider on offer.

Closed Sun. afternoon, Mon. ❖ Credit cards: Visa/CB, Eurocard/Access

---

02310 CHARLY-SUR-MARNE (AISNE)
Calais 352 km – Reims 70 km – Paris 80 km

*MAISON DE
CHAMPAGNE*

**Champagne
Baron Albert**
Grand-Porteron
tel.: 23 82 02 65
fax: 23 82 02 44

The Baron family have been wine growers in Charly since 1677 and today continue the family traditions with the production of a range of wines utilizing, in part, grapes grown on their own 30 hectares of vineyards. Charly-sur-Marne is the birthplace of the fabler Jean de la Fontaine who was a friend of the Barons. Thus the company's de luxe *cuvée* is dedicated in his honour, Cuvée Jean de la Fontaine, a vintage Champagne produced from Chardonnay, Pinot Noir and Pinot Meunier only in the best years.

Closed Sun. Appointment appreciated. Charge for visit includes *dégustation*
❖ Credit cards: Visa/CB, Eurocard/Access ❖ English spoken

2400 CHÂTEAU-THIERRY (AISNE)

alais 340 km – Reims 56 km – Paris 90 km

JOPÉRATIVE DE
HAMPAGNE

ampagne
nnier

, rue Roger Catillon

.: 23 69 13 10

x: 23 69 18 18

Champagne Pannier is a highly regarded cooperative with 230 member grape growers who collectively have some 415 hectares of vines in the Vallée de la Marne, the Montagne de Reims and the Côte des Blancs. The cooperative is dynamic and produces about a million bottles of Champagne annually, 80% of which is sold on the domestic market. The Champagnes have won a number of awards and plaudits in the press and are excellent value.

Egérie is a stylish vintage Champagne produced from a *cuvée* of predominantly Pinot Meunier with roughly equal proportions of Chardonnay and Pinot Noir.

The visit includes an audio-visual presentation, tour of the medieval cellars where some ten million bottles lie ageing, followed by *dégustation* and the possibility of direct sales of Champagne and Champagne accessories.

Open for visits by appointment. Closed Jan. and Feb. The visit lasts approximately one hour and the entrance fee includes *dégustation* and a small *cadeau* ❖ Credit cards: Visa/CB, Eurocard/Access ❖ English and German spoken

0200 COMPIÈGNE (OISE) 🏤

arché   Wed., Sat.

alais 220 km – Amiens 78 km – Arras 108 km

RODUITS DU TERROIR

es Fruits de la
erre

rue d'Austerlitz

.: 44 20 32 80

'*Aujourd'hui les gens recherchent les bons produits d'autrefois,*' says Madame Cristante when we asked her to explain the success of this small shop stocked with a comprehensive range of Picardy specialities and good, fresh farm produce and products. In France, just as elsewhere in the world, people are seeking a return to the purer, simpler foods of yesterday, produced without recourse to industrial methods or chemicals, made by traditional artisan methods to the traditional recipes.

Les Fruits de la Terre provides a direct outlet for the produce and products of *agriculteurs* and local artisan producers. This is the place, therefore, to come for local, seasonal fruits and vegetables; farm-killed, free-range chickens and rabbits; fresh, free-range eggs; unpasteurized milk, yoghurt and *crème fraîche*; local cheeses made from cow's, goat's and ewe's milk; honey; prepared foods like *flamiches, terrines, pâtés, foie gras* and *plats cuisinés*; home-baked *gâteaux* and *tartes*; and much else. There are organic breads made with stone-milled flour, baked in wood-fired ovens; local ciders, beers, and fruit *apéritifs*; excellent *sorbet* made from an abundance of soft fruits from Noyon and surrounds; fish soups from the Baie de la Somme. Indeed, virtually all the specialities of Picardy can be found here under one roof in this friendly shop.

Closed Mon. ❖ Credit cards: Visa/CB, Eurocard/Access

Les Fruits de la Terre, Compiègne

UISINIER-TRAITEUR

ionel Journeaux
2, rue d'Austerlitz
l.: 44 20 32 96

'*Vous désirez ?*' Madame asked, as we hungrily perused the delicious foods on offer. '*Tout est fait maison par mon mari,*' she added proudly. This is an unusual shop, for Monsieur Lionel Journeaux is not a *charcutier* but a *cuisinier*. Indeed, before moving here, he was a chef in his own restaurant in the forest. Now he prepares the same quality, gourmet foods for his discerning and appreciative city customers to take away, ready to eat. In addition to a range of fresh salads and cooked vegetables – *tabboulé, salade aux deux riz, salade niçoise* – and cold meats, *quenelles*, eggs in aspic, freshly cooked *saumon au basilic*, there is always a hot *plat du jour*. Today, for example, *le chef* proposes a delicious-smelling chicken breast cooked in wine with wild *girolles* mushrooms. How we wish we had a house here to which we could take such foods to eat. No matter: Madame can supply the dish piping hot together with plastic knives and forks. So armed, we scamper quickly away to the forest to enjoy this superior meal *en plein air*, followed afterwards with a lovely walk through the woods.

Closed Mon. ❖ Credit cards: Visa/CB, Eurocard/Access

*CONFISERIE-
CHOCOLATERIE*

es Picantins
4, place de l'Hôtel
e Ville
l.: 44 40 05 43

Les Picantins are three figures in medieval attire at the foot of the spire of Compiègne's flamboyant Hôtel de Ville, ready to strike the hours and quarter-hours. Les Picantins in this chocolate shop, on the other hand, are delicious mixtures of hazelnut and nougatine covered in chocolate. They are a local speciality as are Les Duchesses, pieces of candied fruit, macerated in maraschino liqueur and rolled in almonds. Everything here is made on the premises.

Closed Mon.

Shopping for Food and Drink

CAVE À VINS

Cave Nicolas
3, place de l'Hôtel
de Ville
tel.: 44 40 04 97

This centrally located *cave* on Compiègne's main square, virtually opposite the statue of Jeanne d'Arc, is run by a friendly couple, Monsieur and Madame Beaupuis. There is on offer the customarily extensive range of Nicolas wines including, as always, a selection of wines *en promotion*. Also, there is available a particularly good selection of chilled Champagnes, perfect to quench the thirst or spin out the afternoon on an extended *pique-nique* in Compiègne's magnificent forest.

*Jeanne d'Arc,
Compiègne*

Closed Sun. afternoon, Mon.
❖ Credit cards: Visa/CB, Eurocard/
Access, American Express

80500 LE CROTOY (SOMME) 🏛

Marché Tues., Fri.
Calais 98 km – Abbeville 26 km – Boulogne-sur-Mer 64 km

POISSONNERIE

Chez Francine
8, quai Courbet
tel.: 22 27 00 43

Le Crotoy, though today primarily a charming tourist resort, is still a working port and its quayside is lined with fish stalls, many of them manned by the fishermen or their families. Monsieur Francine, for example, is a *pêcheur à pied* – that is, he goes out into the mudflats and marshes of Le Crotoy on foot in search of a harvest from the sea. Sometimes he may pull on his waders and, thigh deep in the tide, drag a net behind him in order to collect the tiny, sweet *crevettes grises*. He also cultivates his own *moules* in the bay. Sometimes he and his family dig for cockles or search the rocks

Samphire

for crabs and goose barnacles. The marshes are an abundant source of the sea plant samphire, known locally as either *passe pierre, haricot de mer* or *salicorne*. This delicious vegetable, out of season, is bottled and conserved, but it is best enjoyed fresh, eaten as an accompaniment to fish. You can prepare it the same way as fresh *haricots verts*, that is, simply steamed or boiled, then lightly dressed in *vinaigrette*, butter or *beurre blanc*.

In addition to what Monsieur Francine gathers or fishes himself, there is always a fairly extensive range of shellfish and fish on offer as well as bottles of the superlative *soupes de poissons* made across the bay in St-Valery.

Open daily

2000 LAON (AISNE) 🏨
Calais 220 km – Amiens 120 km – Reims 58 km

**FROMAGERIE-
CAVE À VINS**

**Fromagerie
Canoine**
5, rue Châtelaine
Tel.: 23 23 53 59

Cheese and wine: the classic French combination. Come to this *fromagerie* in the Haute-Ville for a good selection of both. Monsieur Jacques Canoine offers a well-kept range of regional cheeses including Maroilles, Boulette d'Avesnes and Dauphin plus others from throughout France.
His limited but intelligent selection of wines is far better than that found in most *épiceries* and his prices are reasonable (10% discount for quantities of twelve bottles or more which can be made up in mixed cases).

Closed Sun., Mon. ❖ Credit cards: Visa/CB, Eurocard/Access

BOULANGERIE

**Boulangerie-
Pâtisserie
La Châtelaine**
54, rue Châtelaine
Tel.: 23 20 65 38

Cheese and wine *chez* Canoine, *pain à l'ancienne* from La Châtelaine: what more do you need for a simple *pique-nique* while strolling around Laon's ramparts? All of the excellent breads here are *fabriqués à l'ancienne*, that is, made from dough prepared with a starter and allowed a long, slow rise before baking. In addition to *baguettes* and *pain de campagne* there is a good selection of *pains spéciaux* including *pain aux noix, pain complet, pain de son, pain de siègle*.

Closed Sun.

Shopping for Food and Drink

02170 LE NOUVION-EN-THIÉRACHE (AISNE)
Marché Wed.
Calais 194 km – Avesnes-sur-Helpe 21 km – Cambrai 48 km

FRUIT WINES

**La Chapelle
Jérome**
1, Fontaine des
Pauvres
tel.: 23 97 09 99
fax: 23 98 97 63

Marie-Pierre Gruson and Ferdinand Lapersonne have, since 1988, utilized the soft fruits of their Thiérache farm – *framboises* (raspberries), *fraises* (strawberries), *groseilles* (redcurrants), *cassis* (blackcurrants) and *mûres* (blackberries) – to produce a delightful range of fruit wines under the Folie Douce de Thiérache label. The wines are produced by mixing fresh fruit (single varieties or mixed) with water and sugar, pitching in wine yeast and allowing the mixture to ferment for about a month. The wines are produced in both *demi-sec* and *moelleux* versions by adding, in varying amounts, a *dosage* before bottling. However, as the fruit is very high in fixed acidity, the wines do not actually taste as sweet as you might imagine. Our favourite is Folie Douce Duc de Guise, made from pure raspberries. It is actually quite wine-like with a delicate, raspberry nose and a sharp, refreshing acidity. Folie Douce Cuvée de la Fôret is made from strawberries, raspberries and blackcurrants – a sweet summer pudding of a wine which is delicious served with fruit or dessert such as *tarte aux fraises*.

Marie Pierre and Ferdinand also make a range of *confitures* from their fruits and a refreshing *cidre artisanal*. All of these homemade products are served daily for afternoon *goûter – pâtisserie aux fruits rouges, pain de campagne, confitures* accompanied by tastings of Folie Douce, other fruit wines and fruit syrups for nondrinkers and children.

The full range of products, together with fresh soft fruit in season, can be purchased in the farmhouse shop.

Open for farm visits by appointment ❖ English spoken

60400 NOYON (OISE) 🏛

Festival *Marché de Fruits Rouges* second Sun. in July
Calais 200 km – Compiègne 24 km – Laon 52 km

EPICERIE
FINE-CREMERIE

**Epicerie Fine de
Picardie**

27, place de l'Hôtel
de Ville

tel.: 44 44 10 79

This small *épicerie* opposite the Hôtel de Ville is a good
source of local and regional products: mustards made from
Champagne vinegar, regional *apéritifs*, local cheeses
including Rollot and Maroilles, bottled conserved vegetables,
and much else. There is also *foie gras* and *confit de canard*
from the Périgord and a good range of sausages and *salami*
from Italy.

Closed Mon. ❖ Credit cards: Visa/CB, Eurocard/Access

80200 ST-CHRIST-BRIOST (SOMME)

Calais 168 km – Amiens 50 km – St-Quentin 31 km

FISH FARM

**Le Vivier
d'Omignon**

28, rue de l'Eglise

tel.: 22 84 13 05

At Denis Boulanger's fish farm, located on a network of
canals and rivers between Amiens and St-Quentin, you can
rent a rod and line and fish for the day, enjoy a drink on the
terrace, eat simple meals of fish and smoked fish in season,
even play mini-golf.

    The real attraction, though, is to come here to purchase
superlative, fresher than fresh trout as well as good smoked
trout, eels and carp.

Closed Tue., Jan. ❖ Credit cards: Visa/CB, Eurocard/Access

02100 ST-QUENTIN (AISNE)

Marché Wed., Thur., Fri., Sat.
Calais 174 km – Amiens 75 km – Reims 95 km

CHOCOLATERIE-
CONFISERIE

Jean Trogneux

, rue St-André

el.: 23 62 21 11

Another outlet for the enterprising Trogneux family, this
shop is located just around the corner from St-Quentin's
impressive Hôtel de Ville built in the flamboyant, Flemish
Gothic style. The eighteenth-century belfry that rises from
this large and dominant edifice has a carillon of thirty-seven
bells which chime the hours and quarter-hours most
sweetly (the locals, remarkably, seem no longer to hear

them or to take any notice!). The shop offers the usual range of Trogneux specialities: handmade chocolates and, of course, *macarons d'Amiens*. This shop's particular speciality, however, is the *St-Quentin*, a dark, bitter chocolate in the shape of the head of St-Quentin-de-la-Tour whose portrait graces the French 50 F note.

Closed Sun., Mon. morning

Hôtel de Ville, St-Quentin

80230 ST-VALERY-SUR-SOMME (SOMME)

Marché Sun.
Calais 108 km – Abbeville 18 km – Boulogne-sur-Mer 67 km

POISSONNERIE

Poissonnerie Opale Marée
9, quai Blavet
tel.: 22 60 82 06

St-Valery is definitely a holiday resort, pure and simple. Even mid-week in high season the town can seem curiously quiet. But on weekends and holidays all year round, it explodes into life as city dwellers from Paris and its environs, Amiens, St-Quentin and elsewhere, escape to the sea. Along the waterfront, the bars and restaurants all open, outdoor tables and umbrellas appear and crowds stroll along the promenade which extends along the mouth of the Somme.

This shellfish and fish shop located on the waterfront

only opens at weekends and holidays but then it does a walloping business, selling a good selection of wet fish, shellfish of all types, prepared *plateaux de fruits de mer* to take away ready to eat, smoked *bouffis* and kippers, chilled wines, and a selection of fish and shellfish soups – *soupe de poissons, velouté de coquilles St-Jacques, soupe au langoustines* – that are superlative. Indeed, these fish soups from St-Valery can rival even their famous counterparts from Serge Pérard of Le Touquet across the bay. Purchase them by the pack of six jars to take back home with you for a marvellously concentrated, lingering taste of the sea-fresh essence of northern France.

Poissonnerie Opale Marée, St-Valery-sur-Somme

Open Fri., Sat., Sun. and holidays

60300 SENLIS (OISE)

Marché   Tue., Fri.

Calais 256 km – Paris 40 km – Compiègne 32 km

BOULANGERIE-
PÂTISSERIE

André-Paul Carbonneaux
26, place Henri IV
Tel.: 44 53 49 44

Located in the heart of medieval Senlis, in the main square just down from the cathedral, this artisan *boulangerie* is the place to come to sample the real *pain picard*, a traditional, slow-raised *baguette* made from a mixture of wheat and rye flours: crusty, chewy and delicious. Monsieur Carbonneaux also has a good selection of other breads, *viennoiserie*, and *pâtisserie*.

Closed Sun., Mon.

CHAMPAGNE

While the north of France is not regarded as wine country, we are more than fortunate that Champagne lies just three hours from the Channel Tunnel. For, as the most accessible wine region, it provides outstanding opportunities to purchase excellent quality Champagnes direct from the growers who make the wines themselves.

Champagne is not a cheap wine, nor, if it is any good, can it ever be. If you are simply looking for inexpensive sparkling wines, then there are scores of French alternatives, not to mention well-made sparkling wines from throughout the world. Yet Champagne is Champagne and it remains unique: quite simply, at its best, the greatest sparkling wine in the world and the benchmark against which all others are measured. The best way to appreciate this is to visit the region and learn about the wines at the source.

While undoubtedly the great and famous houses – *les grandes marques* – are the ones which have created the prestige and luxury image that

Moulin à vent, Verzenay

Champagne has long enjoyed, less well known are the literally hundreds of small growers – *les récoltants-manipulants* – who tend the vineyards, sell much of their annual harvest to the large houses but who also lay aside some grapes (they claim the best) to produce their own Champagnes. Certainly, one of the most fascinating aspects of a visit to Champagne is the chance to visit such growers, view their cellars, speak to them about how Champagne is produced, and taste and purchase at the source.

At best, the quality and character of such growers' Champagnes can be outstanding and individual although never as consistent as that of the *grandes marques*. Moreover, it is fascinating to taste and compare growers' Champagnes from different parts of the Champagne region: easy and soft Pinot Meunier-dominated Champagnes of the Vallée de la Marne and the western slopes of the Montagne de Reims; powerful, full-bodied and vinous Champagnes produced from mainly Pinot Noir grapes grown in the classic communes of the Montagne de Reims like Bouzy, Mailly, Aÿ and Ambonnay; and lighter, fresher, more invigorating Blanc de Blancs Champagnes from the Côte des Blancs, produced entirely from the white Chardonnay grapes.

Come and visit *récoltants-manipulants* to learn about Champagne from the small end of the scale and to get to know the wine growers and wine makers themselves. We are certain that you will not be disappointed in the individual quality and character of the Champagnes they produce and that you will soon discover firm favourites.

There are also a number of excellent Champagne cooperatives whose wines have received considerable acclaim in recent years that also warrant visits. Cooperatives have access to the grapes from their members' vineyard holdings, and the best have both the most modern, technological equipment to transform the grapes into well-made wines and the marketing initiative to sell the finished Champagnes nationally and internationally. Such Champagnes are often the most reliable and offer the best value in supermarkets.

The principal shopping motive for a visit to Champagne is, of course, Champagne itself. However, don't overlook the still wines of the Coteaux Champenois (particularly the red wines of Cumières and Bouzy) as well as other local specialities such as marc de Champagne, fine de la Marne and ratafia. Furthermore, both Reims and Epernay have excellent food and drink specialist shops.

Stop to taste; stop to buy

DON'T MISS ...

visiting Champagne growers (*récoltants-manipulants*)
and Champagne cooperatives (*coopératives de Champagne*)

touring *grande marque* Champagne houses

Champagne chocolates (Pierry)

snail farm (Olizy-Violaine)

regional *charcuterie* (Reims and Epernay)

biscuits roses de Reims (Reims)

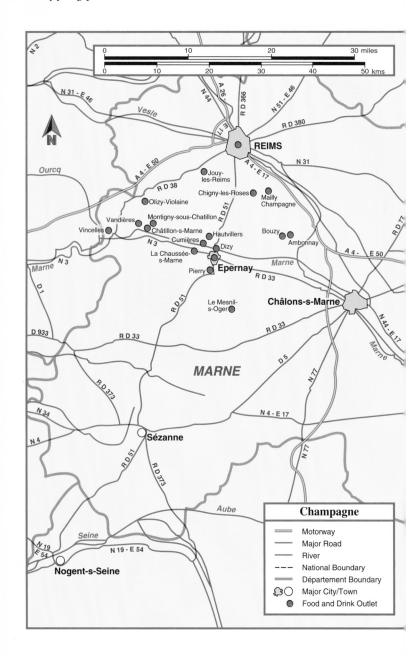

1150 AMBONNAY (MARNE) 🏢

...alais 311 km – Reims 29 km – Epernay 20 km

**...a Palette de
...acchus**

...2, rue St-Vincent
...l.: 26 57 07 87
...x: 26 57 81 74

Ambonnay, like most small Champagne villages, presents a rather dour aspect to the first-time visitor, its stone houses inward looking and closed, its great, secret heritage far underground and out of sight. There are often not even many shops in such towns and the visitor can drive through with something of a sense of frustration at having passed through and missed the essence of the place. Valérie Soutiran's stylish *boutique*, then, is a welcome stop here in this famous wine town in the heart of the Montagne de Reims. It offers a range of Champagnes from both the Soutiran-Pelletier family house as well as from other growers, cooperatives and *grandes marques* alike, including Henri Abelé, Bollinger and H. Blin. Coteaux Champenois still wines from René Geoffroy in Cumières and Herbert Beaufort in Bouzy are also available as well as marc de Champagne, fine de la Marne and ratafia. Additionally, there is an excellent selection of wine accessories including some beautiful, reproduction crystal *flûtes* from the Cristallerie Royale de Champagne, wine buckets, wine stoppers, books and local specialities like *biscuits roses de Reims* and liqueur-filled chocolates.

Come here both to purchase Champagne and accessories as well as to enjoy by the *flûte* or bottle a selection of different Champagnes in the small 'Champagne bar' in the back of the shop. Valérie Soutiran can help to arrange visits to local *caves*.

Credit cards: Visa/CB, Eurocard/Access ❖ English spoken

51150 BOUZY (MARNE)
Calais 309 km – Reims 27 km – Epernay 18 km

RÉCOLTANT-
MANIPULANT

**Champagne
Herbert Beaufort**
32, rue de Tours
tel.: 26 57 01 34
fax: 26 57 09 08

Bouzy is one of the *grands crus* of Champagne, a small village in the heart of the Montagne de Reims with vineyards that face south and southeast and a favoured micro-climate and soil which results in the exceptional fact that the entire aptly named commune is rated 100% Grand Cru. The vineyard is planted overwhelmingly with Pinot Noir grapes which ripen to a high degree and have long been prized by the large Champagne houses for the power and backbone that they lend to the *cuvée*.

The Beaufort family cultivates some 16 hectares of vineyards, 13 hectares of which are planted with Pinot Noir, the remainder with Chardonnay. The ripest, most mature Pinot Noir grapes are harvested separately to be utilized for the production of Bouzy *rouge*. 'These grapes would make a Champagne that is too strong and powerful. But, of course, we need such grapes to make the best red wines. I am experimenting with different clones of Pinot Noir that I have planted specifically to produce Bouzy *rouge*. My hope is that they will give the wines greater colour and tannin. This should improve our red wines in the future.

Monsieur Henri Beaufort's comments are borne out by his wines. The Beaufort Carte d'Or Brut nonvintage, for example, is a classic example of Champagne from Bouzy. Produced primarily from Pinot Noir with some Chardonnay to lighten the wine and add finesse, this is, nonetheless, an immensely full and powerful Champagne which would probably be best enjoyed with food. Beaufort's Bouzy *rouge* Coteaux Champenois (we sampled the 1986 vintage) is rather light in colour, delicate and has perfumed Pinot nose, and a surprisingly well-structured body with round, almost sweet tannins.

Beaufort's Coteaux Champenois, and other examples from Bouzy and elsewhere, are indeed serious red wines, quite unlike Pinot Noir produced anywhere else in the world. The only drawback, admittedly serious, is that because they are produced from the same valuable grapes as Champagne (the most expensive per kilogram in the world), they, too, are always expensive, sometimes even more costly than Champagne. They deserve to be tried, nonetheless.

Closed Sun. Visits to the *caves* by appointment ❖ Credit cards: Visa/CB, Eurocard/Access

---

COLTANT-
NIPULANT

ampagne
ul Bara

ue Yvonnet
: 26 57 00 50
26 57 81 24

Paul Bara is another of Bouzy's small *vignerons* with a large reputation, a *récoltant-manipulant* who, from his 11 hectares of vineyards planted primarily with Pinot Noir with some Chardonnay, produces both outstanding grower's Champagnes and full-bodied, yet delicately perfumed Bouzy *rouge* Coteaux Champenois, utilizing traditional wine making methods.

Bara is a man of Bouzy. His family have been wine growers here for five generations and can trace their ancestry in the town back to 1657.

Open for visits and direct sales by appointment. Closed Aug.

---

700 CHÂTILLON-SUR-MARNE (MARNE) 🏛

arché Wed.

lais 314 km – Epernay 19 km – Reims 32 km

VEAU DE
GUSTATION

ve du Château
de l'Église
: 26 58 42 82
: 26 58 39 62

Châtillon-sur-Marne is dominated by an immense statue of this small wine town's most famous son, Pope Urban II, who in 1095 launched the First Crusade. Urban's view of the Vallée de la Marne and the seemingly never-ending Champagne vineyards is indeed an enviable one, and scores of tourists, coachloads of them in the summer, ascend to enjoy it. This is certainly one of the most visited tourist spots in Champagne but don't let that put you off. Crowds notwithstanding, it is still probably one of the finest *pique-nique* spots that you can find.

Two energetic young Champagne growers, Frédéric Nowack from nearby Vandières in the Vallée de la Marne and Hughues Beaufort from Bouzy in the Montagne de Reims, have created this welcoming tasting *caveau* in the town's main square, cunningly sited so that you have to pass it en route to Urban's viewpoint. But don't worry: this is no tourist clip joint by any means, for both of these serious *vignerons* produce excellent Champagne from their respective vineyards, albeit of different styles. Nowack's fruity and round, is dominated by Pinot Meunier grown in the Vallée de la Marne while Beaufort's, full-bodied, intense and powerful, is made almost exclusively from Pinot Noir grapes from the Montagne de Reims around Bouzy. The full range of Champagnes from both houses is available, Champagnes can be tasted, production methods are explained and the Champagnes are for sale at the same price as *chez le viticulteur*. There are also the superlative Beaufort Coteaux Champenois *rouge* and *blanc* wines, ratafia marc de Champagne and other local specialities. If you would like to visit either property, the staff will help you arrange an appointment.

Open daily ❖ Credit cards: Visa/CB, Eurocard/Access ❖ English spoken

---

51240 LA CHAUSSÉE-SUR-MARNE (MARNE)
Calais 516 km – Reims 54 km – Epernay 7 km

FROMAGERIE ARTISANALE

La Ferme Gourmande
avenue du Dr Jolly
tel.: 26 72 58 22

Jean-Pierre Langlet has a restored Champenois farm where he raises goats and produces an excellent and tasty *fromage de chèvre*. The farm is well set up to receive visitors, and there are guided tours to explain the process of cheese production. There is a shop where the cheeses can be tasted and purchased alongside other *produits régionaux* including local honey, cider from the Aube, *charcuterie* from the Ardennes and locally distilled *eau-de-vie*.

There is also a large *salle* where simple *goûters* are served provided you make a reservation first, including *chèvres chauds*, *salades*, *crêpes*, *gaufres*, *fromage blanc*, *charcuterie*.

Open daily except Jan. and Feb. ❖ English spoken

500 CHIGNY-LES-ROSES (MARNE)
...lais 297 km – Reims 15 km

*...ÉGOCIANT-
...ANIPULANT*

...hampagne Cattier
...rue Dom Pérignon
...: 26 03 42 11
...x: 26 03 43 13

The Cattier family have been *vignerons* in Chigny-les-Roses since 1763 and they have been producing Champagnes under their own *marque* since just after the First World War. While the family owns some 18 hectares of vineyards, all classified Premier Cru, in Chigny and surrounding communes on the northern flank of the Montagne des Reims, this alone is no longer sufficient to meet the company's entire needs. Additional grapes are, therefore, purchased from other smaller growers in the neighbouring localities. This means that Champagne Cattier is classified as a *négociant-manipulant*, though, in effect, the philosophy of the house is more like that of a large grower.

While the Cattier Brut nonvintage, produced from 35% Pinot Noir, 35% Pinot Meunier and 30% Chardonnay, is a classic, firm and gently fruity Champagne, the house pride is undoubtedly its prestige *deluxe cuvée* Clos du Moulin. This is indeed a very special Champagne, one of only four such single vineyard *clos* Champagnes (the others are Krug's Clos du Mesnil Blanc de Blancs, Philliponnat's Clos des Goisses and Bollinger's Vieilles Vignes Françaises Blanc de Noirs). Cattier's Clos du Moulin is in prestigious company indeed.

*...hampagne Cattier,
...higny-les-Roses*

Produced from a walled, single vineyard of only 2.2 hectares, of which half is planted with Pinot Noir and half with Chardonnay, just outside Chigny, it is a Champagne that is made and handled with extreme care at every stage of production, from the harvest and selection of the grapes, to the careful pressing by traditional means and the collection of only the first, finest and most delicate, free run musts. The Pinot Noir and Chardonnay wines are carefully vinified separately, the best selected and blended. As Clos du Moulin is a nonvintage wine, there is a second *assemblage* which takes place, usually from three exceptional and old vintages with a minimum age of at least seven years. For example, the Clos du Moulin that is currently released is an *assemblage* of vintage wines from 1982, 1983 and 1985. After *assemblage*, it further benefits from a long, slow secondary fermentation in the bottle and lengthy aging *sur lie*, being degorged only just before its release. Like all the greatest Champagnes, Clos du Moulin combines rare complexity, power and concentration with great elegance and finesse.

Cattier's *caves*, located in the neighbouring wine commune of Rilly-les-Montagne, can only be visited by groups by appointment (minimum ten persons). Individuals may still wish to drop in on the reception in Chigny to taste the wines at the source and to purchase the rare and prestigious Clos du Moulin and other Cattier Champagnes.

Closed weekends except July–Aug. Groups only for visits to the *caves*, appointment essential ❖ Credit cards: Visa/CB, Eurocard/Access ❖ English and German spoken

51480 CUMIÈRES (MARNE)

Calais 311 km – Epernay 3 km

RÉCOLTANT-MANIPULANT

Champagne René Geoffroy
150, rue du Bois des Jots
tel.: 26 55 32 31

The Geoffroy family has been in Cumières nearly 400 years and for most of that time they have been wine growers. Today, as in the past, René Geoffroy continues the production of grower's Champagnes of great individuality and personality, utilizing methods which have changed very little for decades, if not centuries.

René Geoffroy cultivates 12 hectares of Pinot Noir, Pinot Meunier and Chardonnay grapes in Cumières and th surrounding communes. Once harvested, he lightly presses the grapes in the traditional champenois press, still the best, he feels, to achieve good, clean musts which maintain their essential, varietal character. Geoffroy then, unusually, ferments the bulk of the wines in wood, again a traditional method long abandoned elsewhere but essential to the full, robust house character of the René Geoffroy Champagnes. To preserve freshness and crisp finesse, on the other hand, Geoffroy assembles and bottles the wines before they undergo the malolactic fermentation, another key element in the hand-production of these superlative wines.

né Geoffroy,
umières

Such traditional methods and careful tending by hand result in a range of wines with immense personality, style and tipicity. Even the straight-forward Cuvée de Reserve Brut nonvintage is a wine of considerable character, full, yet with a fresh, lemony acidity and bite that comes, in part, from the fact that malolactic fermentation has not been carried out. Cuvée Selectionée Brut is altogether more serious and profound. Made from an *assemblage* of two-thirds Pinot Noir and one-third Chardonnay, it is a full, biscuity Champagne with some wood notes, yet with an invigorating, underlying grapefruity acidity. The Prestige 1988, a vintage *cuvée* made only in the best years, is made in the reverse proportion of two-thirds Chardonnay and one-third Pinot Noir, vinified entirely in wood. It is fine, light and elegant, yet with a more marked wood character on both nose and palate and has rather rich, warm, brioche-like flavours. Geoffroy's rosé, produced by the traditional method of *saignée*, that is, by leeching the colour from the skins of black grapes prior to vinification (rather than by blending still red wine with white, the more common method), is another noteworthy Champagne, full in colour, intensely fruity when young, more vinous after a few years' bottle age.

Cumières, like the better known Bouzy, is a wine commune also noted for its red Coteaux Champenois wine and Geoffroy's are among the best that we have sampled, produced generally from an *assemblage* of vintages, reasonably deep in colour, yet suprisingly delicate and light with marked Pinot Noir character.

Open for visits by appointment. Direct sales daily

51318 DIZY (MARNE)
Calais 304 km – Epernay 3 km

---

*RÉCOLTANT-
MANIPULANT*

**Champagne Gaston
Chiquet**
BP 1019
890–912, avenue
Général Leclerc
tel.: 26 55 22 02
fax: 26 51 83 81

A friend recently gave us a bottle of Gaston Chiquet Blanc de Blancs d'Aÿ which was, quite frankly, one of the most pleasureable pure Chardonnay growers' Champagnes that we have ever come across: full and rich, yet exceedingly fine at the same time with neither a hint of coarseness nor a touch of that mean, green bite from which wines from this *cépage* can suffer when they are too young. That the grapes were grown in Aÿ, a commune known almost exclusively for the quality of its Pinot Noir grapes, was even more surprising. We had to track down the house, and eventually had the opportunity to meet Monsieur Claude Gaston at his elegant family *maison* in Dizy. He explained to us that his grandfather had been the first to plant Chardonnay in this part of the Montagne de Reims as long ago as 1935 and that the house had actually begun commercializing its own *marque* of Champagnes even before this, in 1920, one of the first *récoltants-manipulants* to do so. Today, Monsieur Gaston and his two sons, Antoine and Nicolas, continue to exploit some 22 hectares of family vineyards planted in Aÿ, Dizy and Hautvillers in proportions of roughly 40% Pinot Noir, 40% Chardonnay, and 20% Pinot Meunier. While we consider the Blanc de Blancs d'Aÿ to be the most outstanding, the Spécial Club vintage Champagnes have also received considerable attention.

Open for visits by appointment

UPERMARCHÉ

:entre Leclerc

l.: 26 55 14 55

x: 26 54 93 03

We don't consider that supermarkets and *hypermarchés* are necessarily the best place to purchase Champagne. The prices of the *grandes marques* are rarely that interesting, and the bargain Champagnes at knockdown prices can be of questionable quality at best. Better by far, we feel, to go direct *chez le viticulteur*. It's more fun, too.

This supermarket, not far outside Epernay, may be useful all the same. There is an excellent in-house *boulangerie*, good *charcuterie*, cheeses, and fresh produce. In addition to Champagne and wines, there is a superlative selection of speciality beers including a good range of Belgium examples: Trappist beers like Orval, Chimay, Rochefort and Westmalle; Lindeman's gueuze, kriek and faro; Grimbergen, Duval, Kwak; and many others, all with their respective beer glasses.

Closed Sun. ❖ Credit cards: Visa/CB, Eurocard/Access

1206 EPERNAY (MARNE)

Marché Tue., Sat.

Calais 306 km – Reims 26 km – Paris 143 km

:AVE À CHAMPAGNE

:hampagne Avenue

5, place de la

.épublique

:l.: 26 55 27 39

ux: 26 51 53 65

This stylish Champagne shop in the centre of Epernay stocks a full range of 120 different Champagnes from both *grandes marques* and *petits vignerons* as well as Coteaux Champenois wines, marc de Champagne, fine de la Marne and ratafia. The proprietor, Monsieur Brochet, says that he looks, above all, for *un bon rapport qualité-prix* at whatever price level. Indeed, his least expensive Champagne, which currently costs 68 F, is a wine of which he is exceedingly proud, made primarily from Chardonnay grapes grown on a tiny, half-hectare plot in Chouilly in the Côte des Blancs. Only 3,000 bottles are made and Monsieur Brochet takes virtually all of them. The wine maker? It is, he admits rather shyly, his own mother.

In addition to Champagne, wines and spirits, you can find plenty of other local specialities here including *biscuits roses de Reims*, *chocolats au marc de Champagne*, flavoured vinegars and mustards made from Champagne vinegar, a full range of glasses, crystal *flûtes*, coolers, Champagne

stoppers, corkscrews and other wine and Champagne accessories, even sabres for decapitating bottles. There are always two wines open for *dégustation*: a *grande marque* at 20 F a *flûte* and a grower's Champagne at 15 F. So if you are feeling thirsty, pop in to say hello and have a drink.

Discounts are available for purchases of more than twelve bottles.

Open daily ❖ Credit cards: Visa/CB, Eurocard/Access, American Express ❖ Some English spoken

Avenue de Champagne, Epernay

FROMAGERIE

Les Délices de la Ferme
19, rue St-Thibault
tel.: 26 55 30 18
fax: 26 58 15 55

Madame Renée France Vautrin offers no less than 150 cheeses, most of them local and produced from *lait cru*, depending on the season. Many of the cheeses that she stocks have won medals at important agricultural fairs. Good local cheeses include Langres, Carré de l'Est, Chaource, Brie de Meaux made from *lait cru*, and *fromage de chèvre cendré et affiné au Champagne*.

'We also consider Maroilles to be one of our local champenois cheeses,' she explained to us, even though that great cheese of the north comes from the Avesnois-Thiérache area of Pas de Calais and Picardy. 'The reason is because, traditionally, the *vendangeurs* came at harvest time from the mining towns of the north and they always brought Maroilles cheese with them. Thus, even today, grape harvesters enjoy Maroilles cheese as a custom during the *vendange*.'

Madame Vautrin travels to the great Paris market at Rungis each week to select her cheeses which she purchases

Les Delices de la Ferme, Epernay

young and finishes ageing in her moist, cool *caves* below the shop. In addition to cheese, she offers farm *crème fraîche crue*, slabs of butter, fresh eggs, local sausages and *pâté*.

Closed Sun., Mon. ❖ Credit card: Visa/CB ❖ English spoken

HARCUTERIE-RAITEUR

u Compagnon de aint Antoine

–3, place Léon ourgeois

l.: 26 55 25 78

This large and busy *charcuterie* is one of the best and most impressive in the region. Monsieur Jean-Marie Gimonnet works with a team of about twenty people to produce daily on the premises an outstanding range of prepared pork products (the full traditional gamut of the *charcutier*) including *pâtés*, *terrines*, *boudin noir*, *boudin blanc*, *hure*, *tête de veau*, *rillettes*, *andouillettes*, *jambonneau*, *jambon persillé*, fresh sausages and much else. The daily output also includes an impressive range of tasty *plats cuisinés* and *plats du jour* which only need to be heated up, lots of good, fresh salads and aspics plus some really delicious cold fish *terrines* and *galantines* including *ballotine aux trois poissons*, *terrine de coquilles St-Jacques*, *saumon farci*. Other outstanding house and regional specialities

include *pâté en croûte, tourte champenoise, feuilleté champenoi* and the famous local *jambon de Reims*. This is certainly th place to come to put togeth a really special *pique-nique champenoise*. There is also a range of quality Fauchon de Paris products on sale including conserved vegetables, mustards, vinegars, as well as a small selection of wines.

Au Compagnon de Saint Antoine, Epernay

Closed Sun. afternoon, Mon. ❖ Cre card: Visa/CB

51160 HAUTVILLERS (MARNE)
Calais 308 km – Epernay 5 km

RÉCOLTANT-MANIPULANT

Champagne J. M. Gobillard & Fils
38, rue de l'Église
BP8
tel.: 26 51 00 24
fax: 26 51 00 18

Hautvillers is, of course, the *berceau de Champagne* – the birthplace of Champagne – and most serious wine lovers will wish to visit this quiet and atmospheric wine town. It is perhaps a pity, then, that such an important monumen as the Abbey of Hautvillers, where the blind cellarmaster Dom Pierre Pérignon perfected the art of Champagne, is not open to the public.

Come here all the same and console yourself with a *coup* of grower's Champagne at the welcoming tasting *caveau* of J. M. Gobillard just opposite the abbey church. In season, visitors are taken to the principal Champagne *caves* in Dizy 1 kilometre away, where they are given a tour followed by *dégustation* of two different Champagnes. Otherwise, the wines can be tasted and purchased at the *caveau* in Hautvillers. The J. M. Gobillard Cuvée Prestige vintage wine is particularly recommended, produced from about 40% Chardonnay and 60% Pinot Noir.

Open for visits and direct sales weekdays; Sat. and Sun. direct sales only
❖ Credit cards: Visa/CB, Eurocard/Access ❖ English and German spoken

*BOULANGERIE-
PÂTISSERIE*

**Boulangerie-
Pâtisserie de
l'Abbaye**
62, rue Henri Martin
tel.: 26 59 40 93

A good bakery with a range of fresh breads all baked on the premises, tasty *pâté en croûte* (excellent picnic fare) and a sensational range of homemade biscuits and cookies including raisin, chocolate chip and the *biscuits roses de Reims*.

Hautvillers

51390 JOUY-LES-REIMS (MARNE)
Calais 290 km – Epernay 25 km – Reims 8 km

*RÉCOLTANT-
MANIPULANT*

**Champagne
L. Aubry Fils**
4 et 6, Grande Rue
tel.: 26 49 20 07
fax: 26 49 75 27

The Aubry family have been wine growers in Jouy-les Reims since the sixteenth century though the family can trace its antecedents back even further. One Aubry de Humbert was the archbishop of Reims who laid the foundation stone for its great cathedral in 1211. An excellent *prestige cuvée* Champagne is named after this illustrious relative.

Today, young brothers Philippe and Pierre continue to cultivate 16 hectares of vineyards planted on the western flanks of the Montagne de Reims. This is a zone, explains Philippe, where Pinot Meunier, the neglected grape of Champagne, thrives well to produce wines with a markedly individual character. L. Aubry Classique Brut nonvintage, for example, is made from predominantly Pinot Meunier and it has a soft, rounded, fruity character allied with an invigorating, underlying freshness that is typical of Champagnes from the western Montagne. More interesting is the Brut Tradition which comes from a select single vineyard (*monocru*) situated in Jouy and is vinified in the classic, traditional manner in small, oak casks resulting in a more robust, biscuity character.

Shopping for Food and Drink

Jouy-les-Reims

The Aubry brothers are great enthusiasts and ambassadors of their region, its history and wines. They are particularly pleased to welcome visitors even without appointments and personally give guided tours, whenever possible, of their fascinating and impressive *caves* which date back in part to the Gallo-Roman era, and explain the traditional aspects of wine making in a small, family Champagne house.

In addition to their range of Champagnes, there are also other local products for sale, including the famous *biscuits roses de Reims*.

Open for visits and direct sales Mon.–Sat.; Sun. by appointment only. Groups welcome by appointment ❖ Credit cards: Visa/CB, Eurocard/Access ❖ English and Italian spoken

51500 MAILLY CHAMPAGNE (MARNE)
Calais 297 km – Epernay 25 km – Reims 15 km

COOPÉRATIVE DE
CHAMPAGNE

Champagne Mailly
Grand Cru
28, rue de la Libération
BP 1
tel.: 26 49 41 10
fax: 26 49 42 27

Mailly Champagne is located in the heart of the prestigious Montagne de Reims vineyard. Out of some 294 wine communes entitled to the Champagne *appellation*, only seventeen are classified as Grand Cru. Mailly Champagne is one such commune and thus each member of this highly regarded cooperative winery possess vineyards classified 100% Grand Cru, planted primarily with Pinot Noir and some Chardonnay. Collectively, the cooperative has at its disposal grapes from some 70 hectares of Grand Cru vineyards.

Champagne Mailly Grand Cru is a cooperative that has been in operation for over sixty years and it is widely regarded as one of the region's finest. Each year, it produces about half a million bottles of distinctive and highly regarded Champagnes. Our favourites include the Mailly Grand Cru Extra Brut produced from a blend of old vintages with only a minimal *dosage*, and the full-bodied, intense and powerful Mailly Grand Cru Blanc de Noirs produced entirely from Pinot Noir.

Open for visits and direct sales Mon.–Fri. and Sat. morning. May–15 Sept. and Nov.–31 Dec. open weekly as above plus Sat. and Sun. afternoon. No appointment necessary. Charge for visit includes *dégustation* ❖ English spoken, and Spanish during the week

51190 LE MESNIL-SUR-OGER (MARNE)
Calais 322 km – Epernay 14 km

RÉCOLTANT-
MANIPULANT
AND WINE MUSEUM

Champagne
Launois Père & Fils
, avenue Eugène
Guillaume
l.: 26 57 50 15
x: 26 57 97 82

Le Mesnil-sur-Oger is located in the heart of the Côte des Blancs, the region south of Epernay planted almost exclusively with the great white grape of Champagne, Chardonnay. Some of the best growers' Champagnes come from the Côte des Blancs because, it is argued, more balanced *monocru* wines can be produced from Chardonnay alone than from either Pinot Noir or Pinot Meunier. Certainly, the best Blanc de Blancs Champagnes are noted, above all, for their finesse and elegance, qualities present in the Champagnes of Bernard Launois. The Blanc de Blancs

Cuvée Réservée nonvintage is a particularly invigorating and fresh Champagne while the Blanc de Blancs 1985 vintage is deeper, richer and more complex.

The Launois family have been *vignerons* in Mesnil-sur-Oger since 1872. Today, Bernard Launois and his wife Dany are happy to receive visitors. They have created a Champagne museum of old wine-making instruments, and casks and presses from the seventeenth, eighteenth and nineteenth centuries. They have a welcoming *salle de dégustation* where groups of between thirty-five and fifty can enjoy wine tastings with a *buffet campagnard*.

Open Mon.–Fri.; weekends by appointment. Charge for visit, which lasts about an hour, includes *dégustation* and a *cadeau souvenir* ❖ Credit card: Eurocard/Access

---

51700 MONTIGNY-SOUS-CHÂTILLON (MARNE)
Calais 312 km – Epernay 15 km

RÉCOLTANT-MANIPULANT

Champagne Charlier & Fils Aux Foudres de Chêne
4, rue des Pervenches
tel.: 26 58 35 18
fax: 26 58 02 31

Jackie Charlier is a grower who is best known not only for his Champagnes and Coteaux Champenois wines produced by traditional artisan methods but also for a highly regarded range of *spécialités champenoises* including ratafia, vieux marc de Champagne, vieille fine de la Marne, fruit such as cherries and raspberries steeped in *eau de vie de Champagne*, and chocolates made with marc de Champagne. Jackie and his wife also have three *gîtes ruraux* available to rent either by the week or weekend, except during the *vendange*.

Open for visits and direct sales Mon.–Fri.; weekends by appointment. Groups by appointment. Visit and *dégustation* of one *flûte* of Champagne is free but charge for visit with more extensive tasting including Champagne, ratafia and fine de la Marne or marc de Champagne

1700 OLIZY-VIOLAINE (MARNE)

Calais 307 km – Epernay 24 km – Reims 25 km

NAIL FARM

**'Escargot de
ħampagne**

, rue de l'Église
el.: 26 58 10 77

Monsieur Bernard Moreau has created a unique snail farm for the *élevage* of fresh, free-range snails which live outdoors and are highly prized by the restaurateurs of the region who use them extensively in a range of regional dishes. In case you have never sampled them, fresh snails, as opposed to rubbery, tinned snails imported to France from abroad, really are a great, flavoursome delicacy. Amateurs of *escargots* may, therefore, wish to visit the farm to purchase them fresh or conserved in jars and supplied with recipes for their preparation. Once a month, Monsieur Moreau holds open house and visitors can view a small snail museum and *escargorium*.

Open for public visits first weekend of each month, 1430–1830. Other times by appointment. Direct sales working hours ❖ A little English, and German spoken

1530 PIERRY (MARNE)

Calais 311 km – Epernay 3 km

'HOCOLATERIE

**a Chocolaterie
ħibaut**

one Artisanale
ue Max Menu
el.: 26 51 58 04
ux: 26 55 39 61

*a Chocolaterie
"hibaut, Pierry*

Monsieur Denis Thibaut is an *artisan-chocolatier* specializing in chocolate *bouchons* filled with marc de Champagne, ratafia and fine de la Marne. The cork-shaped *bouchons* are high quality specialities indeed and many of the finest restaurants of the region serve them after meals with coffee

as a *grand finale champenois*. Though Monsieur Thibaut used to have his workshop in Epernay, the success of his handmade chocolates necessitated a move to this rather dull industrial estate outside town at nearby Pierry. Here, he now has a certain amount of machinery to aid him and he can make up to 60 kilograms of chocolates each day. This is still a labour-intensive operation done by hand, each chocolate 'cork' passing through several production stages before being wrapped in foil ready to be consumed. Come here to see the *atelier*, witness the process, and taste and purchase the chocolates at the source. A word of warning to the bashful: Monsieur Thibaut also specializes in a remarkable range of outrageously rude chocolates.

Closed Sun. ❖ Credit cards: Visa/CB, Eurocard/Access

51100 REIMS (MARNE) 🏢
Marché Daily except Sun.
Calais 282 km – Epernay 26 km – Paris 144 km

BOUTIQUE-
CHAMPAGNE BAR

**La Boutique
Nominée-
Bar Champagne**
place du Parvis
tel.: 26 40 43 85

This Champagne *boutique* is located directly opposite the magnificent cathedral of Reims. If you are only in town for an afternoon, it is a good place to stop to purchase a few bottles or to refresh yourself with a *flûte* of Champagne at the bar as a break from sightseeing. The selection of Champagnes on offer is fairly comprehensive and most of the *grandes marques* are represented as well as wines from some good cooperatives. Prices are fair if not world shattering, especially given the location. As always, the *deluxe* and *cuvée prestige* wines are not discounted but prices of the normal nonvintage Champagnes compare well with the supermarkets. There are always some interesting wines *en promotion* including the well-made range of Champagne Jacquart. Come here, too, for Champagne accessories, glasses or regional specialities such as the *biscuits roses de Reims*.

Open daily ❖ Credit cards: Visa/CB, Eurocard/Access, American Express

---

CHARCUTERIE-
TRAITEUR

Traiteur Martin
32, place Drouet
d'Erlon
tel.: 26 47 33 22
fax: 26 40 92 52

Traiteur Martin is an exceptional *charcuterie-traiteur* particularly worth visiting to put together a superior *pique-nique* to take into the wine country. Naturally, there is a full range of cured pork products on offer (the speciality is a succulent *jambon braisé*) but this centrally located shop is most noteworthy for a delectable range of *plats cuisinés froid* – platters of cold salmon and salad, *terrine de foie gras de canard*, *pâté en croûte*, *mosaïque de légumes au coulis de tomates*, *terrine de lotte et filets de sole, terrine de ris de veau braisé aux poireaux* – accompanied by an excellent selection of freshly prepared salads. Purchase a fine meal here (ask for plastic forks and paper plates), buy a couple of chilled bottles of Champagne either in town or along the sign-posted *Route du Champagne*, then find a nice, secluded picnic spot to spin out the whole afternoon, either in the vineyards of the Montagne de Reims itself or at the lovely Faux-de-Verzy, a unique forest of stunted beech trees in the woods above Verzy on the Montagne de Reims.

Open daily

Traiteur Martin, Reims

ÉPICERIE FINE

a Table en érigord

, place Drouet Erlon

.: 26 47 73 74

Monsieur Alain Ebrard, who comes from Perigueux, runs this stylish *boutique*-restaurant specializing in the *bons produits* of his native region. Specialities of the Périgord produced by Pierre Champion (there are about a dozen such outlets throughout France) include superlative *foie gras de canard* available either fresh (packaged *sous-vide*), *mi-cuit* or *en conserve*; a range of excellent *plats cuisinés* including *confit de canard, cassoulet, potée de périgord, canard à l'orange, civet de sanglier*; plus *eau de vie, liqueurs*, cognac, armagnac, and a good selection of wines from the southwest including a fair selection of sweet dessert wines, the traditional accompaniment to *foie gras*.

Alain Ebrard, La Table en Périgord

There is also a small restaurant where all of the specialiti
on offer in the *boutique* can be enjoyed.

Closed Sun., three weeks in July and one week in Feb. ❖ Credit cards: Visa/C
Eurocard/Access ❖ English spoken

CAVE À VINS

La Vinocave
43, place Drouet
d'Erlon
tel.: 26 40 60 07

La Vinocave is owned by the Champagne house of Alain
Thienot which produces a very creditable nonvintage
Champagne as well as a superlative rosé Champagne; thes
wines are always on offer here at excellent prices, probabl
the best buys in the shop. Though La Vinocave also stocks
Champagnes from most of the *grandes marques*, there are a
few wines from less well known growers simply because
tourists (including the French), explains Monsieur Jacque
Audet the manager, are generally looking for familiar *gran
noms*. Monsieur Audet is knowledgeable but not pushy an
he is always happy to advise customers on good buys in an
price range. There is a particularly good selection of *petits
châteaux* from Bordeaux priced between 30 F and 50 F,
plus Burgundies from Louis Latour and Alsace from Dopl

Au Moulin. There are always wines *en promotion* and a 10% discount is offered for still wines purchased by the dozen, mixed or unmixed.

Closed Sun., Mon. ❖ Credit cards: Visa/CB, Eurocard/Access

OULANGERIE-
ÂTISSERIE

e Four à Bois
), rue de Vesle
l.: 26 47 40 20

e Four à Bois,
'eims

Le Four à Bois, located on the stylish, main shopping street of Reims, actually has a working, wood-fired bread oven in the shop in full view of the customers. Here Monsieur Zunic bakes a range of superlative breads, the most noteworthy of which is *pain aurore*, a superior *baguette* produced with a sourdough *levain* starter, the hand-formed dough having been allowed to rise slowly for a full eight hours before being baked in the wood oven. This is sensational French bread as it should be but all too rarely is these days: the crust hard and crisp, the interior dense, chewy and slightly sour. In addition to this speciality, there is a full range of other speciality breads including *pain aux lardons, pain aux olives, pain au roquefort, pain aux raisins*, plus

a number of *pains biologiques* made from organic, stone-ground flours, including *pain de seigle, pain complet, pain de son* and *pain aux sept céréales*. So good are the breads that it is easy to overlook the range of excellent, homemade *pâtisseries* and *viennoiseries*, all baked on the premises.

Open daily ❖ English spoken

---

*CHARCUTERIE-
TRAITEUR*

**Au Cochon Sans
Rancune**
105–107, rue de Vesle
tel.: 26 47 33 35

Au Cochon Sans Rancune is probably the best *charcuterie* in town for an unrivalled range of regional, cured pork produce as well as fresh pork. Specialities include the full gamut of *charcuterie* products, mostly with a definite champenois accent: *pâté en croûte au lapin, pâté champenois, hure, tête de veau, jambon de Reims, jambonneau, terrine de campagne, terrine de lapin* and prize-winning *andouillettes de Troyes* and *boudin blanc*. This shop is something of a Remoise institution. It has been here since 1902 and everything continues to be made on the premises.

Closed Sun., Mon. ❖ Credit cards: Visa/CB, Eurocard/Access

SPÉCIALITÉS DE REIMS

Biscuits Fossier
25, cours J. B. Langlet
tel.: 26 47 59 84

Fossier is the specialist of the famous *biscuits roses de Reims*, exquisite, pink biscuits baked in a wood-fired oven. As these delightful biscuits are not particularly sweet, they are ideal accompaniments to a *coupe* of Champagne mid-morning or mid-afternoon. In addition, Fossier also produces a range of other sweet Reims specialities, including *pain d'épices au miel* and *massepain*.

Closed Sun.

HYPERMARCHÉ

Carrefour
RN 31–BP 7
Reims-Tinqueux
tel.: 26 48 40 00
fax: 26 84 01 85

This superstore, not far off the A4 *autoroute* (exit Reims-Tinqueux), is not a bad place to stock up on food and drink if you are heading towards the Channel Tunnel on your return home. It is considerably less hectic than anywhere else closer to Calais, and the quality of the fresh produce, *charcuterie* and cheeses is good, if not comparable to the specialist shops in the city centre. Perhaps surprisingly, there is not a vast or overly impressive selection of Champagnes and prices for the *grandes marques* are not necessarily much better than in the *boutiques* and specialist wine shops of Reims. However, the present glut of Champagne means that there are always bargain-basement examples on offer (at the time of writing, for less than 50 F a bottle). Better buys include Champagnes from reliable cooperatives, such as Champagne Jacquard, Nicolas Feuillatte and Albert Le Brun, all priced at well under 100 F a bottle.

In addition to Champagne, there is a fairly extensive selection of table wines, though again, we urge you to resist the temptation to go for the least expensive wines and choose, instead, the safer and more reliable wines within the 20 F to 40 F price range. As well as the usual pallets of Alsace and Belgium lagers, there are some good, specialist beers, most notably the outstanding duo of Belgium Trappists from Chimay and Orval, the former rich and malty, the latter outstandingly bitter and hoppy.

Closed Sun. ❖ Credit cards: Visa/CB, Eurocard/Access

1700 VANDIÈRES (MARNE)
alais 316 km – Epernay 21 km – Reims 34 km

*ÉCOLTANT-
ANIPULANT*

**hampagne
owack**

, rue Bailly
.: 26 58 02 69
x: 26 58 39 62

Frédéric Nowack is a tall, young man with high, striking cheekbones and something of a laughing cavalier's countenance. It is not difficult to believe that one of his ancestors was a Polish officer in the service of Napoleon. Apparently, he stopped here in Champagne, married a local woman from Vandières and stayed long enough to father six children. Then, as quickly as he had appeared, he vanished, apparently returning to Poland to reclaim his inheritance. He was never seen nor heard of again.

The Nowacks have remained in Vandières ever since, continuing the cultivation of grapes, a principal activity for the inhabitants of this small community since Gallo-Roman days. 'The Vallée de la Marne and our stretch of it here in Vandières,' explained Frédéric, 'is the most favourable habitat for Pinot Meunier, a grape that is often overlooked compared with the better known Pinot Noir and Chardonnay. Yet Pinot Meunier at best is capable of making excellent Champagne in its own right. Our Champagnes of Vandières, which are produced predominantly from Pinot

Meunier, are prized, above all, for their fruity roundness.' To test this, we sampled the Nowack Carte d'Or Brut nonvintage made from 100% Pinot Meunier. It is fresh and fruity, with an attractive, green-apple character, a light, easy to drink, delightful Champagne.

Frédéric has supplemented his plantations of Pinot Meunier in the Vallée de la Marne with small parcels of vineyards planted with Pinot Noir in the Montagne de Reims and Chardonnay in the Côte des Blancs. He now works some 8 hectares of vineyards in total and utilizes virtually all of his grapes for his own Champagnes. A relatively new wine of which Frédéric is very proud is the excellent Cuvée Laurine, a Blanc de Blancs made in limited quantity from Chardonnay grapes grown both in the Vallée de la Marne and the Côte des Blancs and named after the Nowacks' six-year-old daughter.

The Nowacks, incidentally offer an extremely pleasant *camping à la ferme* in the garden behind the house and winery. Pitch a tent if you care to and get acquainted with this friendly family and their excellent Champagne.

Open daily for visits and direct sales during working hours except Sun. afternoon. Appointment appreciated but not essential ❖ Credit cards: Visa, CB, Eurocard/Access

Laurine Nowack

1700 VINCELLES (MARNE)

alais 324 km – Epernay 29 km – Reims 42 km

OOPÉRATIVE DE
HAMPAGNE

hampagne H. Blin
t Cie SC
P 35
l.: 26 58 20 04
x: 26 58 29 67

This relatively small cooperative, located in the heart of the Vallée de la Marne, is well equipped and has access to grapes from its members' 90 hectares of vineyards. Champagnes produced are Le Brut Tradition Blanc de Noirs, Le Brut Réserve (80% Pinot Noir and Pinot Meunier, 20% Chardonnay), Le Brut Rosé and, in exceptional years only, the vintage dated Le Millésime. Additionally, H. Blin et Cie produces still wines of the region, Coteaux Champenois *blanc et rouge*, as well as the unique Champenois specialities ratafia, vieux marc de Champagne and vieille fine de la Marne.

As most of its production is sold on the French market by mail order (30% of sales are export), the company is eager to welcome visitors, show them the installations and give them a full tasting of its range of wines.

Open for visits and direct sales daily except Sun. in Jan., Feb. and Aug. Guided visits by appointment. Charge for visit and *dégustation* ❖ English spoken

UPPER NORMANDY

Upper Normandy, which straddles the Seine valley across the *départements* of Seine-Maritime and Eure, is the easternmost part of Normandy, one of the greatest regions of France for fine, regional produce, local specialities, a wealth of farmhouse cheeses and other dairy products, and farm ciders and calvados.

Normandy is, above all, a rich, abundant and generous land which has never had to make do with scratching a regional gastronomy from humble ingredients. Almost every town and locality has its own speciality which visitors come to track down at the source: ducklings from Duclair and Yvetot, cheese and butter from Neufchâtel-en-Bray and Issigny, scallops and sole from Dieppe, tripe from Caen, oysters from St-Vaast and Pourville, cheeses from Camembert, Pont l'Evêque and Livarot, the famous Bénédictine herbal liqueur from Fécamp, cider and calvados from the Vallée de l'Auge, Pays de Risle, Pays de Caux and Pays de Bray, and much else.

Throughout the area covered by this book, there are a number of committed artisan producers: farmers making high-quality Normandy *foie*

Upper Normandy

as de canard et d'oie, farmhouse cheese akers, a rural *boulanger* who, in a ood-fired oven in the Fôret de rotonne, makes the best breads we ave ever tasted, and producers of der and calvados, all of whom can be acked down at the source. There are gn-posted *routes des fromages* and a *ute du cidre*, while eco-museums in the arc Naturel Régional de Brotonne ave exhibitions and demonstrations f how things were done yesteryear (in many cases little different from today). Don't confine yourself to the selection that we have included here: Upper Normandy is a region that deserves far more exploration, so stop to taste and buy whenever you see signs for *vente directe*. And of course, from the smallest villages to the largest towns and cities there is a wealth of small speciality shops which stock the best produce and products from all of Normandy.

DON'T MISS ...

Saturday market (Dieppe)

Neufchâtel cheese (Neufchâtel-en-Bray)

foie gras normand (Bertrimont, La Haye-du-Theil)

Palais Bénédictine (Fécamp)

Musée de la Boulangerie Rurale (La Haye-de-Routot)

parc à huîtres (Pourville-sur-Mer)

Maison de la Pomme (Ste-Opportune-La-Mare)

sucre de pomme (Rouen)

Shopping for Food and Drink

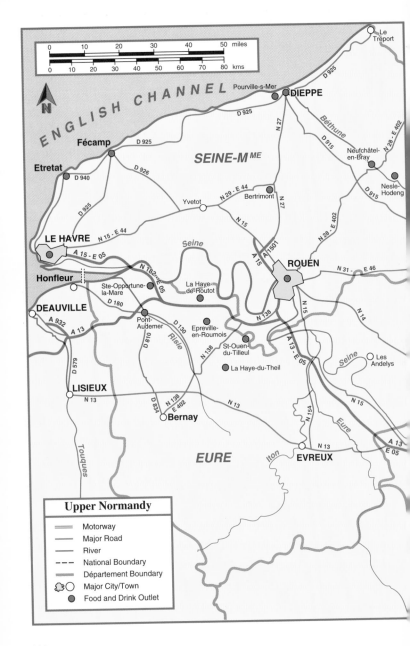

6890 BERTRIMONT (SEINE-MARITIME)

Calais 205 km – Rouen 30 km – Yvetot 20 km

*OIE GRAS
RODUCER*

**a Ferme du
Iisbourg**
el.: 35 32 14 89

Come here for Norman *foie gras* (the speciality is *foie gras mi-cuit*) and other related duck products including *pâté, rillettes, magret de canard, magret de canard fumé* and *confit de canard*, all made on the farm.

Monsieur and Madame Pesquet also offer *goûter à la ferme* consisting of *toasts de bloc de foie gras et de magret fumé, rillette et pâté avec pain de campagne, cidre fermier, dessert, café* or *thé*.

Open for visits and direct sales daily. For visit with *goûter*, telephone first, preferably a few days in advance ❖ English and Spanish spoken

6200 DIEPPE (SEINE-MARITIME)

Marché Tue., Thur., Sat.
Calais 173 km – Rouen 60 km – Le Havre 105 km

*PICERIE FINE-
CAVE À VINS*

'Epicier Olivier
6, rue St-Jacques
el.: 35 84 22 55

Monsieur Claude Olivier may be less well known than his high-profile, younger brother Philippe, of Boulogne and world renown, but he has his enthusiastic devotees as well among the local Dieppoise as well as the scores of British visitors who come regularly to Dieppe for short shopping

Dieppe market

breaks. Claude keeps a discreet but impeccable selection of Norman cheeses in particular, including the local and superlative Neufchâtel (in four different forms), Camembert Livarot, Pavé d'Auge and many others, all purchased from small producers and aged to maturity in his own cheese cellar in the rue des Maillots.

Claude's *épicerie*, though, offers much more than just cheese. There is a range of quality delicatessen foods including the select products of Fauchon de Paris; superlative coffee roasted and ground on the premises; there are fresh fruits and vegetables; and there is a serious wine *cave* with about 350 different wines. Half the range comes from the always reliable Nicolas, the other half is Claude's own personal selection, usually from small, individual *propriétaires-récoltants*. There are always wines *en promotion* and prices are reasonable. Additionally, there is a good selection of regional ciders (*cidre de Pays de Caux, cidre de Pays d'Auge*, and *cidre de Roumois*) as well as a selection of old and extra-old, estate-bottled farmhouse calvados from some of the best small producers such as Roger Groult.

Closed Sun. afternoon, Mon. ❖ Credit cards: Visa/CB, Eurocard/Access, American Express ❖ English spoken

---

**PÂTISSERIE-
CHOCOLATERIE-
TRAITEUR**

Pâtisserie Divernet
138, Grande Rue
tel.: 35 84 13 87
fax: 32 90 08 29

After twenty-seven years on the Grande Rue, Monsieur Divernet, *maître pâtissier, chocolatier* and *traiteur*, has become something of a local institution among the Dieppoise. His shop is the place locals come to when they want to purchase some luxury *pâtisseries* such as a genuine *tarte normande* flambéed in calvados, a super *mercure d'or*, or a gooey *tarte tatin* as well as other cakes, fruit tarts, and handmade chocolates (the calvados-flavoured *le normand* is one of our favourites), all beautifully gift-wrapped, of course, as a superior offering to take to friends or family for dinner or Sunday lunch. Everything is made on the premises including homemade ice creams and *sorbets* as well as savoury *plats cuisinés*. There is a *salon de thé* and pleasant, outdoor tables along the pedestrian precinct where the full Divernet range can be sampled, from a cup of coffee and a pastry or a bowl of ice cream, to simple snacks and lunches. It is a useful place to remember when you don't feel like a full midday meal.

ICERIE FINE

ivre et Sel
1, Grande Rue
.: 35 82 08 76

Madame Nasset, the young owner of this stylish gourmet food and drink shop, has recently moved her premises to the Grande Rue and continues to offer the same range of quality, luxury foodstuffs, including a selection of the excellent Comtesse du Barry products of the southwest. Come here, then, to purchase *foie gras mi-cuit*, *terrines*, *confit de canard*) as well as some good *plats cuisinés* packaged in foil, glass jars or tins and excellent for taking back home as gifts.

She also has a small but interesting range of wines including some good sweet wines to accompany *foie gras* and some interesting and reasonably priced *vins de pays*. There are also wine accessories, wine glasses, a selection of old calvados, cider and malt whiskies. Just about everything – except salt and pepper.

Closed Mon. morning

Poivre et Sel, Dieppe

HARCUTERIE

arcuterie Duhoux
, rue St-Jacques
.: 35 84 18 69

Every *charcutier* worth his curing salt has at least one speciality of which he is most proud. For Monsieur Michel Duhoux, it is undoubtedly that most prized and expensive of all products of the *charcutier*'s art, the *boudin blanc*. Indeed, Monsieur Duhoux's shop is lined with trophies that he has won in various competitions. In 1987, his *boudin blanc* was judged to be the very best in Europe, no mean feat considering that virtually every *charcutier* in France was competing. *Boudin blanc*, for those who have not encountered it before, is a sort of luxury, white pudding made of finely ground, lean pork and finely ground chicken breast, mixed with milk, eggs, salt and pepper, put into a natural casing, then gently poached. It is, thus, already cooked and only needs to be gently reheated.

Perhaps our tastes are basically more rustic. We must admit that the celebrated *boudin blanc* has never been one of our favourites, irrespective of whether it is Monsieur Duhoux's or anyone else's. It is so delicate, so bland that to us it positively smacks of nursery food; indeed, our baby Bella loves it. No, we prefer the more robustly flavoured *boudin noir*, excellent barbequed in summer, or the gutsy yet flavoursome *andouillette* and Monsieur Duhoux's delicious, prize-winning examples are among the best.

Closed Sun., Mon.

CHARCUTERIE-TRAITEUR

Charcuterie-Traiteur Béguet
22, Grande Rue
tel.: 35 84 12 03

This stylish and large shop at the start of Dieppe's most important shopping street is the best place in town to come for a good selection of prepared pork *charcuterie* (excellent *terrines* and *pâtés*) as well as for other more elaborate, prepared cold foods and fresh salads for superlative picnic by the *quai* or on the wide expanses of grass behind Dieppe's promenade. There is usually cooked, free-range chicken, good rare roast beef, a small selection of cheeses plus chilled wine, water and cider, even homemade *pâtisseries* for dessert.

Open daily in season, closed Mon. out of season

BOULANGERIE-PÂTISSERIE

Boulangerie-Pâtisserie Ch. Demanneville
69, rue St-Jacques
tel.: 35 84 22 54

It is not always easy these days to find an artisan *boulanger* which still makes bread in the old way, that is, utilizing a *levain* starter and having the patience to allow the bread to benefit from a long, slow rise. Come here, then, to sample excellent *pain au levain*, nicely sour and chewy, and the sweeter but still flavoursome *bannette*. There are also some good speciality breads, such as the twisted *fougasse*, as well as a selection of breads made from whole grain cereals (*pain aux six céréales, pain de siègle, pain de son*).

'PERMARCHÉ

ammouth
C du Val Druel
: 35 82 65 50
: 35 06 12 67

Hypermarkets anywhere near Channel ports are, to our way of thinking, best avoided but if you are a masochist, this is probably the best in town, although on a busy day the most torturous. It is a vast shopping complex with the usual precinct that includes not only the enormous Mammouth itself but some twenty other small shops. It is located outside town on the road to Rouen.

Closed Sun. ❖ Credit cards: Visa/CB, Eurocard/Access ❖ *Bureau de change* located in the shopping centre

'310 EPREVILLE-EN-ROUMOIS (EURE)

alais 253 km – Rouen 35 km – Pont-Audemer 22 km

JER AND CALVADOS
ODUCER

ançois Bocquet
âteau La Boise
.: 32 56 26 40

As *Commandeur des Goustes Cidre* in a gastronomic organization formed to publicize and defend *les boissons issues du jus de pomme et du jus de poire,* Monsieur François Bocquet is in a position to know what makes a good farm cider, perry, pommeau or calvados. Each year, he organizes important competitions in the *départements* of Eure and Seine-Maritime. He is an enthusiast and a true amateur of these traditional Norman beverages. Certainly, his own examples rank among the region's best. Monsieur Bocquet's Calvados Château La Boise Pays de la Risle, for example, was rated highly in a tasting in *Decanter* magazine. Come here to taste and purchase them at the source.

Open for visits by appointment

76790 ETRETAT (SEINE-MARITIME) 🏛

Calais 243 km – Le Havre 28 km – Fécamp 16 km

FROMAGERIE
ARTISANALE DE
CHÈVRE

Le Valaine
Manoir de Cateuil
route du Havre
tel.: 35 27 14 02
fax: 35 29 23 92

The Dherbécourt family, on their farm in the lush
pastureland of the Pays de Caux behind Etretat's sweeping
cliffs, raise a herd of some sixty goats whose milk is utilized
from March to November for the production of a range of
excellent farmhouse *fromages de chèvre*. The difference
between the cheeses lies entirely in the amount of time that
they have been allowed to age. For example, *fromage blanc*
a type of goat's cottage cheese, sold the same day it has be
made; *fromage frais*, moulded but still very white, soft and
fresh, is meant to be consumed within days of making whi
doux is cheese about ten days old. The longer the cheeses
age subsequently, the harder, drier and more pungent the
flavour, from the still soft, three-week-old *fleuri* cheeses,
through the *affiné* cheeses that are about a month old, to th
sec cheeses which are over two months old and hard,
crumbly and rather acidic in the mouth.

In addition to cheese, there are also some other interestir
farm products which can be sampled and puchased.
The Dherbécourts utilize their goat's milk to produce a
fascinating range of ice creams which are exceedingly ligh
and delicious, most notably an exceptional one flavoured
with calvados. There is also a *terrine de chevreau* on offer,

'Gamin', Le Valaine

their own *cidre* from the Pays de Caux (incredibly rasping scrumpy, definitely something of an acquired taste), milder *cidre* from the Pays d'Auge, farmhouse distilled calvados from the Pays d'Auge and excellent organic wines from the Château Le Barradis in Monbazillac.

Shop open daily March–Nov. Guided visits Easter–30 June and 1 Sept.–11 Nov. on holidays and Sun. at 1100; July–Aug. on Sun., Mon., Tues., Wed. and holidays 1100. Charge for visit includes *dégustation*

NTE À EMPORTER
'S FRUITS DE MER

Huitrière
ont de Mer
.: 35 27 02 82

retat

This excellent restaurant at the end of Etretat's promenade sells *fruits de mer* platters to take away. Though the prices may be somewhat higher than if you simply purchased the equivalents from a *poissonnerie*, at L'Huitrière they will carefully prepare and pack your shellfish for you to take away ready to eat on a super *pique-nique* on the cliffs. You can purchase a dozen or two of *fines de claires* which will be opened for you, a fresh, boiled crab or lobster, full *plateaux de fruits de mer*, all carefully prepared, cracked and presented on a bed of ice in foil containers. And if you still don't fancy

doing it yourself, you can come here throughout the day for a simple *dégustation* of *huîtres* or *fruits de mer*, accompanied by good house Muscadet.

Open daily except Mon. out of season ❖ Credit cards: Visa/CB, Eurocard/ Access, American Express, Diners ❖ English spoken

---

76400 FÉCAMP (SEINE-MARITIME)

Marché Sat.
Calais 227 km – Le Havre 40 km – Dieppe 66 km

LIQUEUR DISTILLERIE

Palais Bénédictine
BP 192
110, rue Alexandre
Le Grand
tel.: 35 10 26 00
fax: 35 28 50 81

Put your hand up if you thought Bénédictine was made by monks? Nope, we're all wrong, not a cassock to be seen. This incredible, bombastic, neo-Gothic palace, one of Upper Normandy's most visited tourist attractions, is a complete pastiche, though none the worse for it. Alexandre Le Grand the founder of the distillery, thought up the idea at the end of the last century of reviving a herbal liqueur once made by monks at the long defunct Abbey of Fécamp. He somehow managed to acquire rights to the recipe, gathered fragments from the ruined abbey such as the old rood screen, statues, illuminated manuscripts and books, and built the *palais* as means of drawing attention to the monastic origins of the drink: a classic example of ingenious, nineteenth-century marketing and entrepreneurial skill.

Make no mistake: his creation is well worth visiting. Visitors see Le Grand's collection of medieval art, paintings, sculptures, ivory, enamels and wrought iron, and view exhibits demonstrating how Bénédictine established itself worldwide and was subsequently copied fraudently in scores of unlikely countries. In the Plant and Spice Hall, the aromas of the twenty-seven plants, roots and herbs from around the world used to produce the liqueur are overwhelming, and you can touch, rub and smell them. The distillery itself can be walked through to see where the lines of copper pot stills are in use, as well as the great, oak casks necessary for the lengthy marrying of essences and maturation of the liqueur. Finally, the unguided tour ends with the chance to taste either a generous measure of Bénédictine, B & B (Bénédictine blended with cognac) or cocktail made with the liqueur.

There is a shop which, of course, sells the products, together with a range of other related items including Bénédictine chocolates, bottles in commemorative tins, boxes and buckets, glasses, trays and ice buckets. As most of these are promotional items, the prices are actually quite keen, so this is not a bad place to pick up gifts to take back home with you.

Open for visits 20 March–28 May 1000–1200 and 1400–1730, 29 May–12 Sept. 1000–1800, 13 Sept.–14 Nov. 1000–1200 and 1400–1750, 15 Nov.–31 Dec. 1030 and 1530 ❖ Shop accepts all credit cards

Palais Bénédictine, Fécamp

6600 LE HAVRE (SEINE-MARITIME)

Marché   Tue., Thur., Sat.

Festival   *Fête du Pêcheur*   first weekend in Sept.

Calais 284 km – Rouen 86 km – Paris 204 km

CHOCOLATERIE-
PÂTISSERIE-
BOULANGERIE

**Chocolatier-
Pâtissier Houlé**
45, rue de Paris
.: 35 41 39 76

Monsieur Houlé has been making fine *chocolats* in front of his customers for some thirty years. Come here between January and November to visit the *atelier* to witness the hand production of specialities such as the *boulette d'or* (a crunchy *feuilleté praliné* covered with dark chocolate) and the *oscar* (named after Oscar Niemeyer, the Brazilian architect who designed Le Havre's strikingly futuristic cultural centre) to take home as gifts. Throughout the year there is also a range of good artisan *pâtisseries*, homemade

sorbets and tasty breads including excellent, chewy *pain au levain* and *pain comple*

Closed Sun., Mon. ❖ Credit card: Visa/CB

Le Havre

CHARCUTERIE-TRAITEUR

Traiteur-Charcutier Duval
127, rue Victor Hugo
tel.: 35 42 42 94

Duval, located on the central place Gambetta, is probably the best *charcuterie* in town. It is the source of not only a full range of prepared pork products but also excellent, ready-to-eat *plats cuisinés*, hot *plats du jour*, fresh cold salads, *tartes* plus a small selection of chilled wines and *cidre*: in short, virtually everything you need for an excellent *pique-nique* either on the ferry or in the lovely and relaxing Fôret de Montgeon located above the Basse Ville which can be reached by funicular, an immense, protected area of great natural beauty with open space where the people of Le Havre go for relaxation in evenings and weekends.

Closed Sun. afternoon, Mon. morning ❖ Credit card:Visa/CB

FROMAGERIE

Cheinisse
Centre Commercial
des Halles Centrales
tel.: 35 21 35 95

Le Havre's covered market, located just off the place Gambetta, is really a collection of excellent, specialist food shops and so deserves a visit, not least to seek out this fine *fromagerie*. Monsieur Claude Cheinisse offers an intelligent and well-kept selection of not only Norman cheeses almost exclusively from small farm producers utilizing *lait cru* but also cheses from throughout France including some good examples from Burgundy, the Jura and Savoie (Epoisses, Comté, Tome de Savoie).

In addition to this cheese shop, the Halles Centrales has a good poultry specialist, La Volaillerie St François, which offers free-range poultry and spit-roasted chickens, a coup of fruit and vegetable stalls, two *poissonneries*, a small supermarket, a *boulangerie* and a Nicolas wine outlet.

Closed Sun.

ISSONNERIE

issonnerie Vérel
rue de Paris
: 35 42 46 33

Michel Vérel's famous fish shop is located just a few paces up from the ferry port and is the source of impeccable, seafresh *fruits de mer – crevettes, huîtres, moules, crabes, langoustines*. Should you wish to take some shellfish home with you on the boat, bring a cool box. Monsieur Vérel is happy to supply the ice. The locals come here to purchase, above all, an exceptional range of fish brought in daily by local boats, particularly the magnificent, local flat fish, *sole* and *turbot*, which are always in demand.

Closed Sun., Mon.

Poissonnerie Vérel, Le Havre

Shopping for Food and Drink

CAVE À VINS

La Générale des Vins
92–92 bis, rue Dicquemare
tel.: 35 22 90 90
fax: 35 42 06 41

This useful and reliable, city-centre wine warehouse specializes in wines from an association of about a dozen small *propriétaires-récoltants*, individual wine growers with whom the proprietor, Monsieur Jean-Pierre Malécot, has exclusive rights to distribute their wines throughout Normandy. The selection, though not vast, is intelligent and manageable and is not overly weighted towards Bordeaux notwithstanding the fact that, as Monsieur Malécot points out, some 70% of wine drunk in Normandy is claret. '*C'est bizarre*,' he shrugs, 'we have such good fish and shellfish here, yet we Normans do not drink much white wine. In summer, we probably drink more rosé than white.'

The Rhône, Loire, Alsace are also well represented, as are Champagnes from *grandes marques* and *récoltants-manipulants* alike, plus minor country wines and other *vins pays*. Prices are extremely competitive with a mark-up, claims Monsieur Malécot, of only 40% (a bottle that costs 10 F at the château costs 14 F here). There are always wines *en promotion* as well as a selection of ten bag-in-box wines.

Monsieur Malécot says that he will offer a 5% discount to purchasers who show him this guide.

Closed Sun., Mon. morning ❖ Credit cards: Visa/CB, Access/Eurocard, American Express

---

HYPERMARCHÉ

Auchan
avenue du Bois au Coq Prolongée
tel.: 35 54 71 71

Located in the Haute Ville in the direction of the Fôret de Montgeon, this is an immense superstore and shopping complex with some fifty shops.

Closed Sun. ❖ Credit cards: Visa/CB, Access/Eurocard

7370 LA HAYE-DU-THEIL (EURE)

alais 252 km – Pont-Audemer 32 km – Brionne 15 km

OIE GRAS
PRODUCER

omaine de la
oudraye
.: 32 35 52 07

Luc and Paulette Damaegdt raise ducks, geese and other poultry on their beautiful, 200-hectare Norman farm and claim that they were the first in the region, about a dozen years ago, to begin the production of Norman *foie gras de canard et d'oie*. Their products are, indeed, of the highest quality so if you, like us, are particularly fond of this great French delicacy, it is worth coming here to track it down at the source.

Duck or goose, that is the question. Though *foie gras d'oie* is the older and more traditional product, it has certainly been something of a fashion in France in recent years to prefer *foie gras de canard*. For our tastes, we find that duck liver is, perhaps, more perfumed and finer than goose liver which is more richly unctuous. As always, it is a matter of personal taste. The Damaegdt's *foie gras* – whether duck or goose – is *mi-cuit*, that is, it is preserved at lower sterilisation temperatures than traditional, conserved *foie gras*, thus maintaining finer, purer flavours. However, do bear in mind that *foie gras mi-cuit* needs to be refrigerated even while in transit. So if you are planning a visit here to stock up you should bring a cool box with you. Once home, Luc advises that jars be stored in the refrigerator and the contents consumed within six months of the date of making.

Visitors who telephone in advance can enjoy a *dégustation* of the classic combination, *foie gras*, toast and a glass of Sauternes. There are also oven-ready, free-range chickens, guinea fowls, turkeys and capons for sale, though to be sure that they are available when you arrive, you should telephone your order in advance.

Open for visits and direct sales Mon.–Sat. Closed Sun. Groups welcome by appointment ❖ Credit card: Visa/CB ❖ English spoken

---

76270 LA HAYE-DE-ROUTOT (SEINE-MARITIME)
Calais 256 km – Rouen 38 km – Pont-Audemer 20 km

MUSÉE DE LA BOULANGERIE RURALE

Le Four à Pain
tel.: 32 57 07 99

Faluche brioches, Le Four à Pain

The importance of the village *boulangerie* in French life even today is paramount as most households require fresh *pains* or *baguettes* not just once but at least twice, even three times a day. The *four à pain* is a nineteenth-century, rural bread oven in a typically Norman cottage, dating from the French Revolution, which has been faithfully reconstructed. It is fired up at least once a week for the baking of a range of superb breads and *brioches*.

This eco-museum, under the auspices of the Basse-Seine and Parc Naturel Régional de Brotonne, is not, however, just a picturesque recreation of yesteryear. Monsieur Claude Dambry, who looks after the *four à pain* and gives animated discussions on the history of rural baking, is himself a master *boulanger* and has been in the trade since he was fourteen years old. The range of breads, *brioches* and other specialities that he makes is quite simply outstanding

and well worth a detour to sample. For example, when we visited the *boulangerie* there was *pain au cidre*, a whole-wheat, sourdough bread made with farmhouse cider instead of water. It is flavoursome and chewy with a hard crust and a tangy, sour flavour. This is undoubtedly one of the best breads we have tasted in France! Monsieur Dambry explained that normally, after the breads have been cooked, the *boulanger* would make *brioches* in the cooling oven. He had that morning himself so baked a traditional, Norman brioche known as *faluche*, made with a quarter butter and three-quarters *crème fraîche*. Finally, at the end of the day or overnight, other items might be cooked in the *four* such as *teurgoule*, a type of rice pudding made with rich milk, flavoured with cinnamon and left in the low, still cooling oven for upwards of six hours until the mixture is thick and creamy. Our eight-month-old baby, Bella, loved this traditional, regional speciality, lukewarm straight from the oven.

The *four à pain* is open for group visits and bakery workshops by appointment. Claude Dambry also offers *nuits du boulanger* whereby groups of ten to fifteen individuals can enjoy an evening in the bakery, including a meal of foods cooked in the *four à pain* accompanied by local cider.

Open July–Aug. daily 1430–1830, May–June and Sept. weekends and holidays only, March–April, Oct.–Nov. Sun. and holidays only. Group visits all year by appointment

---

6270 NEUFCHÂTEL-EN-BRAY (SEINE-MARITIME)

Marché   Sat.
Calais 173 km – Dieppe 35 km – Rouen 45 km

ÉPICERIE FINE

Au Palais du Fruit
et 3, rue des
Cordelières
Tél.: 35 93 00 42

Neufchâtel-en-Bray is the centre of the Pays de Bray, an exceptionally rich and fertile pasture and the home of one of Normandy's great cheeses, Neufchâtel. Good examples can be purchased in this small grocery and fruit shop, just off the town's place de l'Église, together with excellent fruit and vegetables and a selection of wines and farmhouse ciders.

Closed Sun.

**FROMAGERIE
ARTISANALE**

*5 km S.E. at
Nesle-Hodeng*

**Ferme des
Fontaines**

tel.: 35 93 08 68

Neufchâtel is Normandy's oldest cheese, made since 1035 by artisan methods that have remained virtually unchanged. Neufchâtel benefits from an *appellation d'origine contrôlée* which ensures that it can only be made within a small, specific area and, indeed, there are only twenty or so individual producers entitled to do so. Come to this welcoming farm located in the heart of the Pays de Bray to see how it is produced and to taste and purchase it at the source.

Here, Monsieur and Madame Brianchon have a herd of fifty brown and white, Norman cows, the unpasteurized milk from which is utilized each day to produce 200–800 cheeses. The milk, once coagulated, is drained overnight in muslin cheesecloths hanging from the ceiling and the fresh cottage cheese that results is then salted and lightly pressed. The curds are broken up and mixed together with a mature bloomy cheese to make a homogenous paste of a consistency not unlike that of bread or pastry dough. This process serves to 'seed' the *pâte* with necessary bacteria to

*Madame Brianchon,
Ferme des Fontaines*

assist development of its rich flavour and characteristic, downy, white rind as it ages. Next, unlike most cheeses whereby the curds have already been left to drain in shaped moulds, Neufchâtel is formed by hand into a variety of different shapes utilizing old-fashioned, metal utensils not unlike giant cookie cutters. This is, indeed, a fascinating process to watch as Madame Brianchon vigorously packs by hand the fresh, white curds into heart shapes, squares, rectangles and cylinders. The *briquette*, *carré* and *bonde* all weigh 100 grams, the *double bonde* and *cœur* (the most popular form of all) weigh 200 grams and the *gros cœur* weighs 600 grams. It takes 1 litre of milk to make the small cheeses and a full 6 litres to make the 'big heart'. Once formed, the cheeses age in moist *caves* wherein the rind ripens and the characteristic, downy bloom and deep flavour develop. Young Neufchâtel can be enjoyed within a fortnight of production while *demi-affiné* cheeses are sold after three weeks and *affiné* cheeses from one to three months.

Open for direct sales daily. Appointment for visits to the cheese dairy preferable but not essential provided it is not too busy ❖ English spoken

---

27500 PONT-AUDEMER (EURE)

Marché   Mon., Fri.

Calais 268 km – Honfleur 25 km – Rouen 50 km

CHOCOLATERIE

Espace Chocolat
16, rue de la
République
Tel.: 32 42 78 78

This excellent *chocolaterie* is a good source of homemade chocolates to take home either to enjoy yourself or to give away as gifts. Don't miss the local specialities: *mirlitons*, *les plaisirs de Pont-Audemer*, *les brindilles de la forêt de Brotonne*, and *pommes calvados*.

Closed Sun., Tue. ❖ Credit card: Visa/CB

Espace Chocolat, Pont-Audemer

Shopping for Food and Drink

76550 POURVILLE-SUR-MER (SEINE-MARITIME) 🏢
Calais 180 km – Dieppe 6 km

PARC À HUÎTRES

L'Huitrière
rue du 19 août
tel.: 35 84 36 20

The Huitrière is a *parc à huîtres* where oysters are cultivated in the bay then purified before being sold to private customers and restaurateurs alike. This is *the* place to purchase a tub of the freshest oysters you will ever eat, either to enjoy immediately or to take back home with you. In summer, a tub will keep for at least three days. In winter the oysters should be fine for about a week. On arriving home consume as soon as possible or keep in the fridge. If you don't fancy opening the oysters yourself, then enjoy a *dégustation* of a dozen or so on the terrace overlooking the sea, with a chilled bottle of Muscadet *sur lie*.

Open daily

76000 ROUEN (SEINE-MARITIME) 🏢
Marché Tue., Wed., Fri., Sat.
Calais 218 km – Amiens 114 km – Le Havre 86 km

FROMAGERIE

Fromages de Tradition
Les Halles du Vieux Marché
place du Vieux Marché
tel.: 35 88 72 13

There have probably been market traders in Rouen's place du Vieux Marché for centuries as this central square has long been at the heart of life in the old city. Today, the small

Place du Vieux Marché, Rouen

covered market, which is part of the modern, architectural complex constructed after the war incorporating the sweeping, slate-roofed construction of the Église de Jeanne d'Arc and the monument to France's national patron saint, carries on this tradition with a clutch of excellent shops as well as outdoor stalls selling fruit and vegetables, superb fish and, of course, Norman cheese and butter. Monsieur

Philippe Jollit, a *fromager-affineur*, has been here for the past seventeen years, and specializes, above all, in fine, Norman cheeses purchased from small, individual producers who make their cheeses from *lait cru*. He chooses the cheeses young then oversees them to ripeness and maturity, ensuring that Camembert *fermier*, Neufchâtel, Pont l'Eveque, Pavé d'Auge and Livarot all reach his customers in perfect condition. If you require cheeses to eat in, say, a couple of hours, a couple of days or next week, ask Monsieur Jollit or his daughter for advice. There is, furthermore, an intelligent selection of cheeses from throughout France as well as rich, yellow unsalted, semi-salted and salted butter cut from the slab and tangy *crème fraîche* from the Pays d'Auge.

Closed Sun. afternoon, Mon. ❖ Credit card: Visa/CB

POISSONNERIE

Poissonnerie Massif

1, rue Rollon
Tel.: 35 71 54 36

This excellent *poissonnerie* offers an outstanding range of wet fish and shellfish, brought in fresh each day from Fécamp and Britanny as well as live lobsters and a variety of superior *plats cuisinés* made fresh every day, such as *taboulé de poisson*, *praires farcis*, *empereur au coulis d'homard*, *filet de cabaillaud sauce vinaigrette* and much else. If, by chance, you are staying in one of Rouen's central *chambres d'hôtes* with kitchen facilities then *profiter* and enjoy a simple feast *chez vous*.

Closed Sun., Mon.

CAVE À VINS

Nicolas

8 bis, place du Vieux Marché
Tel.: 35 71 56 10

Nicolas is just about the only national chain of wine shops in France, their equivalent to our Threshers or Victoria Wine if not quite Oddbins. This is a useful outlet, nonetheless, with an always reliable and comprehensive range of French wines. As always, there are wines *en promotion* each month which are usually interesting and certainly keenly priced. Monsieur and Madame Chalot, the managers, are a friendly and helpful couple.

Closed Sun. afternoon, Mon. ❖ Credit cards: Visa/CB, Eurocard/Access, American Express, Diners ❖ A little English spoken

Shopping for Food and Drink

CHOCOLATERIE

Chocolaterie Richart
16, rue Rollon
tel.: 35 88 18 14
fax: 35 88 45 76

Talk about designer chocolates, Richart's are literally works of art. We have never encountered more beautiful or innovative forms and designs, nor more imaginative, if slightly bizarre flavours, produced, of course, from the highest quality ingredients. There are some forty different varieties including chocolates flavoured with nutmeg, malt whisky, Japanese green tea, and thyme. This is French chocolate *par excellence*, bitter or very bitter. Most of the chocolates contain a minimum of 75% cocoa solids. There are even examples made from 100% cocoa, completely unsweetened and to our taste virtually inedible. The chocolates are sold in beautifully presented gift boxes and make very special presents. And for the chocoholic who has everything: a temperature-controlled *cave à chocolat* made out of beautiful, polished hardwood. Cost? A mere 2,200 F for the smallest version.

Closed Sun. afternoon, Mon. ❖ Credit cards: Visa/CB, Eurocard/Access, American Express, Diners

---

FROMAGERIE AND
PÂTES FRAÎCHES

Fromagerie Leroux
40, rue de l'Hôpital
tel.: 35 71 10 40

This long-standing cheese shop, centrally located on one of old Rouen's charming *rues pietonnes*, is well known not only for the excellent selection of over one hundred cheeses aged in the medieval *cave* below the shop but also for a good selection of *épicerie fine*, quality foodstuffs, including farm chickens, calvados *fermier*, and excellent, fresh pasta and stuffed ravioli made daily. Two other local specialities worth picking up here include *sucre des pommes* (sugar made from apples) and *moutarde jaune forte* (strong brown mustard) made traditionally by Monsieur Tabouelle of Caudebec-les-Elbeuf.

Closed Sun., Mon. ❖ Credit cards: Visa/CB, Eurocard/Access, American Express

VE À VINS

ves Jeanne d'Arc
, rue Jeanne d'Arc
: 35 71 28 92
: 35 15 14 83

uen

Monsieur Michel Blaiset is both *maître encaveur* and *négociant-éleveur*. His wine and spirits shop, located in the heart of the old city, has a fascinating range of mature claret and burgundy purchased *en primeur* and aged in the company's *caves* at nearby Croisset. The entire wine range is indeed comprehensive, from simple *vins de pays* at no more than 12 F a bottle to Château Petrus 1947 at 7,500 F and Château d'Yquem 1937 at 8,400 F. The Blaiset family, furthermore, has vineyard holdings in the classic heart of Burgundy and can offer exclusively wines from its own *domaine*: Beaune Blanche Fleur, Vosne-Romanée Les Chalandins, Chambolle-Musigny Aux Combottes, Savigny-lès-Beaune Les Gollardes, Nuits-St-Georges Les Longecourts. There is a good selection of Loire wines as well as examples from all the classic wine regions of France (Alsace, Rhône, Champagne, Beaujolais, the Jura). The rest of the world, in typical French style, is represented by a pitiful five wines, one of which is a retsina! But there is a good selection of magnums and half-bottles.

The main ageing cellars lie at the nearby riverside suburb of Croisset (8, quai de Danemark, tel: 35 36 55 77) in natural *caves* hollowed out of the chalk cliffs which rise from the banks of the Seine. The range at Croisset is not as comprehensive as in this Rouen city centre shop but, nonetheless, for those wishing to purchase large quantities of wines to take back home, it may prove to be the more convenient outlet.

Closed Sun., Mon. morning ❖ Credit cards: Visa/CB, Eurocard/Access ❖ English spoken

---

27680 STE-OPPORTUNE-LA-MARE (EURE)

Marché   Marchés aux Pommes   first Sun. of each month Nov.–April
Festival   *Fête de la Pomme*   first Sun. in Nov.
Calais 268 km – Rouen 50 km – Pont-Audemer 9 km

APPLE MUSEUM

Musée sur l'Histoire de la Pomme–Vente de Produits Pomologiques
Parc Naturel de Brotonne
tel.: 32 42 47 00

The Parc Naturel Régional de Brotonne is an extensive, protected woodland located in the heart of Upper Normandy.

Musée sur l'Histoire de la Pomme, Ste-Opportune-La-Mare

straddling the Seine in both the *départements* of Seine-Maritime and Eure between Le Havre and Rouen. It is an area of great peace, charm and natural beauty and deserves to be visited. As a means of documenting the history and traditions of the zone's inhabitants, there are a number of eco-museums which can be visited. This apple museum, for example, is located in an old *presbytère* dating from 1710 which served as the house for the priest who taught the children of Ste-Opportune. The museum traces the history and production of *cidre*, pommeau and calvados. There is an explanatory video in English as well as French, a reconstructed cellar and, outside, an old, horse-drawn cider mill that is still used once a year during the *Fête de la Pomme* in early November.

Open July–Aug. daily (except Tue.) 1430–1830; March–June and Sept.–Oct. Sat., Sun. and holidays only 1430–1830; Nov.–Dec., first Sun. of each month 1400–1830. Entrance fee includes *dégustation.* Sale in the shop of *cidre*, pommeau, calvados and local apples in season

---

670 ST-OUEN-DU-TILLEUL (EURE)
lais 242 km – Rouen 24 km

DER AND
LVADOS
ODUCER

**maine des Hauts
nts**

s Hauts Vents
: 35 87 70 11

Monsieur Caboulet is a *propriétaire-récoltant* who produces high quality *cidre*, pommeau and calvados entirely from apples grown on the estate of his sixteenth-century manor. While there are zones in Normandy more famous for the production of these typical and delicious products, the Pays de la Risle is highly regarded, nonetheless. Come to the farm to taste and purchase direct. Monsieur Caboulet is always happy to welcome serious *amateurs* and to explain the artisan production of these famous products of the apple. There is a shop located in the old *pigeonnier*.

Open for direct sales Sat. and Sun. working hours in summer. Other times by appointment

BELGIUM

For the lover of food and drink, Belgium is famous, above all, for two fine things: handmade chocolates and an outstanding range of beers. There are many more fine things to eat and drink as well but no visitor to the country will wish to miss the opportunity to sample, in all their variety, a selection of the best examples of these two most famous products.

Belgian pralines have been produced since the middle of the last century and they remain one of the great specialities of the country, popular not just with visitors but with the Belgians themselves. Each man, woman and child consumes no less than 12.5 kilograms of chocolate a year which works out at about half a pound of chocolates per person per week on average: some national sweet tooth! Of course, we all have our own personal favourites and half the fun is finding out for ourselves what they are.

No other country on earth offers a greater variety of types and styles of beer than Belgium. From the dark, strong and pure beers from five Trappist abbey breweries to the quenching, sour lambics of the Senne valley; from slightly cloudy beers brewed from wheat to glistening, golden 'specials' rich in flavour and alcohol; from malty, fruity, amber brews to vivid, red beers made with fresh, sour cherries; and from classic pilsner lagers known throughout the world to beers from tiny breweries that are rarely encountered outside their own brewery doors: Belgian beers are quite simply astounding in their variety and quality. Definitely something for the connoiseur, Belgian beers are very reasonably priced and one of the best bargains to bring back in quantity.

The Belgians love to eat as much as they love to drink. Therefore, wherever you go, and certainly in all the major towns, there is an excellent range of fine, specialist food shops — *pâtisseries, charcuteries, poissonneries,* delicatessens, bakeries and much else. We have covered a few of the principal towns, such as Brugge, Gent and Brussels, as well as a few other country venues where we think

Burg, Brugge

dependent visitors might care to go. But we stress that we have hardly scratched the surface and this is an area that will warrant much further research in future editions.

Belgium, to date, has been a country that has been curiously neglected, something of a surprise considering that it is such an interesting and varied place literally on our own doorstep. From a food and drink shopping point of view, we are certain that now and in the future there will be many more of us crossing over for regular beer and chocolate runs at the very least. In the process, we will discover, we are sure, much more that the country has to offer.

DON'T MISS ...

handmade Belgian pralines

Musée de la Gueuze (Brussels)

Trappist breweries (Westvleteren and Chimay)

Gent mustard (Gent)

Gantse mokken and *pepperbollen* (Gent)

speculoo biscuits (Brussels)

jambon d'Ardennes

Chimay cheeses (Chimay)

National Hop Museum (Poperinge)

550 BEERSEL (BRABANT) 🏚

alais 216 km – Brussels 10 km

JEUZE BREWERY

**ud Beersel
ouwerij**

arheidestreet 230

.: (02) 380 44 48
(tavern)

(02) 380 33 96
(brewery)

*enri Vandervelden,
ud Beersel Brouwerij*

Belgium is a country for beer lovers and, without a doubt, the most distinctive, unusual and individual beer of all is gueuze, produced by a spontaneous, wild fermentation in a handful of artisan breweries located in the Senne valley of Brussels and its surrounds. The little town of Beersel once supported some sixteen breweries. Today, this is the only one still in operation. Here Henri Vandervelden carries on almost single-handedly the artisan brewing traditions started by his grandfather in 1882. Using the ancient, original equipment, old tools and chestnut barrels which elsewhere would be in a museum of rural life, he still manages to produce a fascinating range of lambic specialities. The Oud Beersel gueuze, for example, is individual and outstanding, like an unsweetened amontillado sherry in colour with a pronounced sour-yeasty nose and tart palate overlayered with deeper, rounder flavours. The Oud Beersel kriek, called Sherry Poesy, is made with the

addition of fresh, sour cherries to provoke a vigorous secondary fermentation, resulting in a strong, perfumed, beautifully foaming, yet raspingly sour beverage.

While visits are, in theory, only available for groups, individuals who telephone in advance can usually join an existing tour. Alternatively, come to Beersel to sample and purchase these specialities in the rural tavern adjoining the brewery.

Open for group visits Easter to end of Oct. by appointment. Individuals by appointment. Otherwise, the beers can be sampled in the adjoining tavern
❖ English, French, Dutch and German spoken

Shopping for Food and Drink

DELICATESSEN

**Marco's
Delicatessen**
Herman Teirlinckplein 2
tel.: (02) 377 00 33

The Pajottenland, the country where Pieter Bruegel found inspiration for his Flemish landscapes and lively peasant scenes, is excellent country for leisurely touring. There is actually a sign-posted *Route de la Gueuze* which leads through lovely countryside with wide, open fields, large, Flemish farmhouses, narrow, winding roads and typical towns and villages. The route extends from Halle in a circuit through Vlezenbeek, Gaasbeek, Sint-Martens-Lennik around to Lombeek and Lennik. Following this is a most pleasant way to spend a day or an afternoon, touring either by car or, better still, by bicycle. You can pick up provisions at this excellent delicatessen in the Beersel town square for a superlative picnic to enjoy along the way – good *charcuterie* and cheese, freshly prepared salads, rare roast beef, roast chickens (at weekends), sandwiches, hot or cold *plats cuisinés* and, of course, Oud Beersel gueuze.

FARMHOUSE
COTTAGE CHEESE

De Kaashoeve
Lotsestraat 43
tel.: (02) 331 06 45

The most characteristic taste of the Pajottenland is *plattekaas* – fresh *fromage frais* made from unpasteurized milk, served as a drinking snack along with a slice of buttered bread and a pile of radishes and spring onions on the side to munch while sipping tumblers of tart, refreshing gueuze. Come to this farm at the entrance to the town to purchase the cheese which is always sold with a bunch of radishes, as well as good farmhouse butter and yoghurt.

Closed Sun., Mon.

000 BRUGGE (WEST FLANDERS)

Market   Wed., Sat.

alais 106 km – Brussels 97 km – Gent 49 km

HOCOLATE SHOP
ND WORKSHOP

**hocolaterie
ukerbuyc**

atelymestraat 5
l.: (050) 33 08 87
x: (050) 33 08 87

*hocolaterie
ukerbuyc, Brugge*

Sukerbuyc means sugar belly in old Flemish and, indeed, this special chocolate shop is something of a temple to all things sweet and beautiful. Here on the premises, Roland Depreter produces a most outstanding and extensive range of the finest Belgian pralines every day. This is fresh chocolate of the highest quality. It is fascinating to taste the different types available: cream-filled, chocolate-filled, fresh cream, liqueur cream, nut, mint cream, truffle, butter chocolates, marzipan and much else, some sixty different types of chocolates in all.

These are true, handmade products, almost works of art in their own way. Yet we discovered how easy it is to devour a box in only minutes! We asked Roland if he himself eats chocolates. 'Yes, all day long. It is actually a problem,' he said with a frown, patting his own *sukerbuyc*.

Roland's wife oversees the shop as well as the hand-production of a beautiful range of marzipan sweets. The couple have been making chocolate and marzipan on the premises for the last sixteen years. Customers are very welcome to have a peep inside the chocolate workshop, if it is not too busy, to see how it is all done by hand, chocolate by chocolate.

Open daily ❖ No credit cards but all foreign currencies accepted, even coins ❖ English, Dutch, German, French and Spanish spoken

Shopping for Food and Drink

CHOCOLATE SHOP

Van Tilborgh
Noordzandstraat 1B
tel.: (050) 33 59 04

In a town where virtually every street has at least one and often several chocolate shops, we consider Van Tilborgh to be among the most outstanding. Ingrid Liebeert is simply passionate about chocolates and she personally ensures that hers are handmade to the highest standards utilizing only first-quality Callebaut chocolate and a range of other top-quality ingredients including the best hazelnuts, almonds, fresh cream, butter and caramel. Rarely do you encounter chocolates this fresh, this intense, this subtle. The house speciality is *paardekopjes* (horses' heads), finely detailed and filled with praliné. These are truly exceptional. Indeed, regular customers flock here to buy them by the kilo. Ingrid's window displays are beautiful and even the hand-packed boxes are individually decorated with a small flower.

'Fresh chocolates are completely different from factory-made chocolates,' advises Ingrid. 'The sooner you eat them the better, the more intensely flavoured they are. They must be kept cool and dry but never placed in a refrigerator which would kill their flavour and make them lose their

Chocolaterie Van Tilborgh, Brugge

shine and beauty. Certain chocolates, particularly those made with fresh cream ganache with no addition of liqueur, for example, may last for no longer than ten days. Butter creams, on the other hand, can last well for four to six weeks provided they are stored properly. So it is always important to ask for advice when purchasing chocolates so that we know both what your taste is and when you plan to consume the chocolates.' We can personally guarantee that if you have some Van Tilborgh chocolates, you need never worry that they won't be eaten quickly enough!

Closed Tue. ❖ Credit cards: Visa/CB, Eurocard/Access, American Express ❖ Dutch, French, English, German and Spanish spoken

---

ELICATESSEN

eldycke
ollestraat 23
.: (050) 33 43 35
x: (050) 33 45 21

This is Brugge's finest delicatessen by far and the place to visit to put together a superior picnic to take to the gardens around the Minnewater, on a walk around the town ramparts or on a bicycle trip along the canal tow path to Damme. There is a full range of Belgian cheeses and meats, including exceptional, smoked Ardennes ham carved off the bone, good salamis and *pâtés*, plus a large range of prepared salads, canapés, stuffed vegetables, cold salmon and other main course dishes which make excellent, knife-and-fork picnic fare. There are also good breads and rolls and the helpful staff will make up any type of sandwiches that you require. Our favourite is a French loaf filled with the exceptionally sweet, tiny, hand-peeled *crevettes grises*, the grey shrimps from the North Sea which are such a delicious, local delicacy.

Mr and Mrs Deldycke, the owners, are always on the premises and will help with any special requirement you may have. Complete picnics can be ordered in advance (in person, by telephone or fax) and these will be packed for you in an English wicker hamper to take away with you for a deposit. Mr Deldycke will even arrange bicycles for you to hire if you so require.

Closed Tue. ❖ Credit cards: Visa/CB, Eurocard/Access, American Express, Diners ❖ English spoken

Shopping for Food and Drink

WHOLE-GRAIN BAKERY

De Trog Volkoren Bakkerij
Wijngaardstraat 17
tel.: (050) 33 31 37

This wholefood bakery is conveniently located on the main pedestrian route that leads to the peaceful Beguinage and Minnewater so it is always well patronized by foreign visitors making a beeline to these beauty spots. There is an extensive range of good whole-wheat and whole-grain breads – sesame, sunflower seed, raisin, ten cereals and much else – all baked on the premises, and a good range of wholefoods, cooked vegetarian snacks, Belgian cheeses and homemade tarts. This is a good place to pick up home-cooked breads and tasty snacks to enjoy sitting by the banks of the lovely, so-called Lake of Love.

Closed Sun. in summer, Thur. in winter ❖ English spoken

CHEESE SHOP

Diksmuid Boterhuis
Geldmuntstraat 23
tel.: (050) 33 32 43

Mrs Willems's *boterhuis* is probably the best cheese shop in Brugge and offers an exceptional range of farmhouse cheeses from Belgium, France and Holland plus good meat and other *charcuterie* from the Ardennes. Her father started the shop some sixty years ago. She herself has been here for at least half that time. The aromas of cheese and smoked meats is a particularly pleasant and pungent mix.

Closed Sun.

BREWERY

De Gouden Boom
Langestraat 45
tel.: (050) 33 06 99
fax: (050) 33 46 44

De Gouden Boom is the principle brewery in Brugge and the source of two outstanding and distinctive beers: Brugs Tarwebier, the famous *blanche de Bruges*, a quenching, sour, wheat beer usually served in stout tumblers, and Brugse Tripel, a deceptively pale but potent, top-fermented ale served in a tall, elegant glass which best displays its glistening colour. De Gouden Boom, located in the heart of old Brugge, is still very much a working brewery and there are no facilities for visits by individuals. However, you can often join group tours if you call or write as far in advance as possible. Visits to the brewery last about one and a half hours and the tour ends with a glass of beer.

Open for guided visits daily except Sun. and public holidays. Appointment needed, preferably in writing at least a week in advance. Charge for tour includes a glass of beer ❖ English, French, Dutch and German spoken

REWERY

**ausbrauerei
traffe Hendrik**

Jalplein 26

l.: (050) 33 26 97

x: (050) 34 59 35

Unlike De Gouden Boom, the Straffe Hendrik is well placed to receive visitors. There are daily tours of the small, working brewery, and, best of all, there is a large and welcoming beer tavern where the outstanding Straffe Hendrik beer is served along with simple snacks. This is a serious, working brewery which has functioned on these premises since 1856 and still utilizes water from the original artesian source.

The brewery tour is interesting and worthwhile if you have the time. At the very least, don't miss the opportunity to drop in here en route to or from the Minnewater for a welcome rest, a goblet or several of the potent and delicious brew and a bowl of outstanding *biersoep*.

Open daily with guided brewery tours at 1100 and 1500 without appointment
❖ English spoken

Straffe Hendrik brewery, Brugge

Shopping for Food and Drink

Super Delhaize
Malesteenweg 234
tel.: (050) 35 59 48

If you are wondering where to buy beer in Brugge, don't bother with the speciality shops in the city centre. Beer, after all, is not considered a speciality here but virtually a daily necessity. Do as the locals, then, and stock up at this excellent supermarket located outside town on the old road to Gent. There is an outstanding and extensive selection of Belgian beers from throughout the country at very competitive prices, by the bottle or 24-bottle crate, as well as a good selection of reasonably priced wines plus fresh produce and excellent cheeses and *charcuterie*.

Closed Sun. ❖ No credit cards but English money accepted

Beguinage, Brugge

000 BRUSSELS
1arket   daily (various venues)
alais 205 km – Brugge 97 km – Lille 105 km

HOCOLATERIE

euhaus

alerie de la Reine 25–29

l. & fax: (02) 512 63 59

'euhaus, Brussels

Belgian chocolates are known and loved throughout the world but Belgian pralines as we know them originated in this famous confectionary shop in the Galerie de la Reine which has been in continuous operation since 1857. At that time, Jean Neuhaus produced on the premises candies as well as cough drops, liquorice drops to cure heartburn, violet-drops, other home remedies and, as a sideline, some bars of dark chocolate. It was his son, Frederick, who gradually turned the business more towards sweet confections and away from pharmaceuticals, eventually producing moulded, chocolate shells that could be filled with different mixtures. Thus were born the first filled Belgian chocolate pralines.

Today, in Neuhaus's modern factory outside Brussels, *maîtres chocolatiers* produce annually some 3,000 tonnes of pralines using in part the same artisan and hand methods developed over a hundred years ago. The chocolates are distributed to some fifty exclusive Neuhaus shops throughout Belgium as well as to select outlets throughout Europe and the world. This original shop, then, remains something of a mecca for chocolate lovers who will not be able to resist stopping here to sample such classics as gorgeous chocolate truffles (coffee, Champagne, rum and many more), *caprices* (chocolates filled with mixtures of *crème fraîche*, *nougatine* and vanilla), *tentations* (chocolates filled with mixtures of *crème fraîche*, *nougatine* and coffee), *millenaires* (chocolate, *gianduja*, caramel and crisped rice enrobed in chocolate), or moulded *dollars* filled with raspberry or vanilla cream.

Credit cards: Visa/CB, Eurocard/Access, American Express ❖ English spoken

---

**PÂTISSERIE-
CHOCOLATERIE**

Wittamer
place du Grand
Sablon 6–12
tel.: (02) 512 37 42
fax: (02) 512 52 09

On the whole, the most exclusive, high-class shops in Brussels are located in the upper town, and the most exclusive, high-class *pâtisserie*, it is generally agreed, is Wittamer, located in the chic Grand Sablon. When the people of Brussels really want to impress, when only the best will do, they make their way up here.

Founded in 1910 by Henri Wittamer, the firm is still wholly a family business. Come here to admire, sample and purchase such beautiful creations as the famous *tutti frutti*, *cappucino* cake, *passionata* as well as a range of *petits fours*,

individual fruit *tartes* and *éclairs*, mousses, candies and cakes of virtually every description.

This discreet and elegant shop also has a good range of breads and *brioches*, sandwiches and savouries. The chocolate shop, located a few doors down at Grand Sablon 6, has an extensive and highly regarded range of fresh, handmade chocolates of the highest quality.

Wittamer, Brussels

Open daily ❖ English spoken

TRAITEUR

**Boutique du Grand
Cerf**
rue du Grand Cerf 22
tel.: (02) 511 44 93

Brussels has no shortage of really topnotch food and drink shops. This stylish *traiteur* located in the upper town near the Palais de Justice ranks with the best. It offers an outstanding range of prepared, cold and hot gourmet foods prepared daily, to take away ready to eat: *foie d'oie frais*, *foie gras de canard*, *terrines*, *saumon au dill*, *raviolis de homard*, *carpaccio de bœuf*, *coq au riesling et nouillettes*, *choucroute de poissons à la moutarde* and much else. There is a range of excellent *plats du jour* available every day as well as superlative *pâtisseries et desserts maison* so you can put together complete gourmet meals without having to lift a finger except to carry the nicely wrapped packages away. There is, furthermore, a good range of classic wines on offer as well as other luxury foods, conserves, mustards, oils and the like.

Closed Sun., Mon., July ❖ Credit cards: Visa, Eurocard/Access, American Express, Diners

---

SCUITERIE

scuiterie Dandoy

, rue au Beurre

.: (02) 511 03 26

x: (02) 511 81 79

Established in 1829, Dandoy claims to be *la plus ancienne biscuiterie belge* – the oldest biscuit shop in Belgium. Indeed, they say locally that Dandoy's *speculoo* gingerbread figures are as much a part of the city as is the Mannekin-Pis (the famous statue of a little boy caught unashamedly short, usually dressed these days in one of 341 quite ridiculous costumes). A visit to this old-fashioned shop, located between the Bourse and the Grand' Place, is a must,

therefore, not only to see the immense, sometimes life-size gingerbread *speculoos* formed by hand in beautiful, carved, wooden moulds but also to sample them and other specialities such as *pains d'amandes*, *pains à la greque*, *pain d'épices* and *macarons*, all made by hand on the premises and sold fresh every day. The marvelous aromas that emanate from the back of the shop on entering are irresistible.

Open daily

Biscuiterie Dandoy, Brussels

175

Shopping for Food and Drink

FRESH LIVE EELS

Aalvis N.V.
42 quai au Bois à
Brûler

The old fish market area by the defunct *quais*, a
neighbourhood now packed with scores of fish restaurants
remains the centre of the wholesale and retail fish trade,
and both restaurateurs and private individuals come here
purchase live lobsters, crabs, *moules* and, at this unique
specialist shop, live eels. *Anguilles* or to give them their
Flemish name *paling* are, after all, one of the great national
delicacies of Belgium, especially when prepared in green
sauce as *anguilles au vert* or *paling in 't groen*. At this shop
there are tanks containing literally thousands of them, all
squirming and glistening away. Come here to see the eels
and, if you dare, to purchase them yourself to take back
home.

Closed Sun., Mon.

GUEUZE BREWERY-
WORKING MUSEUM

**Le Musée
Bruxellois de la
Gueuze**
Brasserie Cantillon
rue Gheude 56
tel.: (02) 520 28 91
521 49 28

Of all the marvellously varied and rich brews of Belgium,
the most unusual is undoubtedly gueuze, a unique lambic
beer produced by spontaneous, wild fermentation. Before
the First World War, there were as many as fifty gueuze
breweries actually located within Brussels city centre.
Today, Cantillon is the only working brewery left in the
capital. Beer lovers should definitely take the trouble to
make an appointment to visit this remarkable, working
museum located in the Flemish suburb of Anderlecht.

Gueuze, as well as other beers within the same family,
such as kriek, framboise and faro, is produced from lambic
a beer that is brewed from a wort made of 65% malted
barley and 35% wheat, boiled together in the brewing
copper with a high concentration of aged hops. Once the
wort has been separated from the hops, it is pumped into a
open, flat, copper cooling receptacle located in the attic of
the brewery. The attic itself has louvres and vented roof
tiles so that, as the night air from the Senne valley passes
through, wild yeasts and organisms are deposited on the
wort to cause a spontaneous fermentation with no addition
of yeast whatsoever. The next day, this liquid is transferred
to wooden casks and the vigorous, natural fermentation
begins. The fermented beer that results is lambic and is
further aged in wooden barrels for one, two or three years.

asserie Cantillon,
derlecht

Gueuze is a mixture of one-year-old lambic and mature, three-year-old lambic, blended but unfiltered, then bottled in Champagne bottles, sealed with corks and wired down. The young lambic adds sharp vivacity to the finished beer while the aged lambic contributes roundness, complexity and deeper, wood flavours. Moreover, the young lambic still contains unfermented sugars so that after a few months in the bottle, a natural, secondary fermentation occurs which gives the beer its sparkle and foam. This is gueuze and will continue to improve and develop in the bottle for upwards of two or three years, even longer say aficionados. For those who have never tasted real gueuze, as opposed to commercial versions more usually available, it is a remarkable drink: incredibly tart, even sour, yet deep in colour, rich in flavour and marvellously wine-like.

Kriek is another great and unusual speciality. At the end of each July, a harvest of sour cherries from nearby Schaerbeek is brought to the Cantillon brewery. Some 150 kilograms of fresh cherries are pitched into each barrel containing 500 litres of young lambic. The cherries provoke a vigorous, secondary fermentation and also add distinctive fruit flavours and colour. Kriek, like gueuze, is bottled in Champagne bottles and eventually comes out a foaming, vivid red colour. But make no mistake, this is no cherryade beverage for wimps. Real kriek as only available from artisan breweries is unbelievably sour, rasping, refreshing, a magnificent summer drink. Framboise is similarly produced with the addition of fresh raspberries, making it more delicate and perfumed, while faro is made by blending candy sugar and caramel with lambic.

The full range of outstanding Cantillon beers can be purchased in three-bottle packs or by the crate. However, do bear in mind that gueuze is delicate and transporting it by car in heat can cause the beers to begin to ferment, even in some cases to blow their tops. Once home, let the bottles rest on their sides in a cool place (not the refrigerator) and carefully pour off the sediment before drinking.

Open to the public mid-Oct. to the end of April Sat. 1000–1700, weekdays by appointment. Public brewing sessions on the Sat. before 11 Nov. and the last Sat. in Feb. or the first in March. Entrance fee includes tasting, and the beers available for sale

---

6480 CHIMAY (HAINAUT)

Calais 218 km – Brussels 95 km – Avesnes-sur-Helpe 30 km

EPICERIE FINE

Au Cœur des Pres
rue Rogier, 1
tel.: (060) 21 25 26

While the Abbey of Scourmont, producer of Chimay beer lies somewhat outside the town towards the French border, Chimay itself is a fascinating town that deserves to be visited in its own right. Park outside and tour the medieval centre on foot. This useful shop, located at the entrance to the town, offers the full range of Chimay cheeses (six

Abbaye de Scourmont, Chimay

different varieties including an outstanding, beer-washed version) plus all the Chimay beers, good *charcuterie*, and a small range of prepared *plats froids*.

Closed Thur.

FÉ-BAR-BEER SHOP

km S. at
ourmont

berge de
teaupré

Poteaupré 5
.: (060) 21 14 33

Chimay is probably the best known of Belgium's five genuine Trappist beers, brewed at the Abbey of Scourmont near Bourlers and widely distributed nationally and even internationally. Though the abbey can be visited, the brewery itself is off limits and there is no direct outlet for the purchase of either beer or Trappist cheeses. Instead, this nearby country inn serves that purpose, offering the full range of Chimay beers with Chimay cheese and other local products such as *escaveche*, farm butter, bread, honey and much else.

The lightest of the Chimay ales comes in the red-top bottle and has an alcohol content of 6° per volume. This is, nevertheless, a full, malty brew. The white-top is a degree stronger and is lighter in colour, a top-fermented, high-density, special ale. Most distinctive of all, however, is the outstanding blue-top which, at 8°, is a rich, strong, well-hopped and well-balanced beer of great character and distinction. In addition to the usual range, there are occasionally special brews on offer, usually in 75-centilitre bottles, including Grande Réserve and Cinq Cent. The beers are available by the six-pack or 24-bottle crate and are sold at favourable prices. The distinctive Chimay beer glasses, as well as trays and other accessories, can also be purchased.

Open daily in July–Aug., otherwise closed Mon. ❖ Credit cards: Visa/CB, Eurocard/Access ❖ English spoken

9000 GENT (EAST FLANDERS) 🏠

Market   Fri., Sat.

Festival   Gent Festival   about third week in July

Calais 172 km – Brussels 56 km – Brugge 49 km

---

*PÂTISSERIE-
TEA ROOM*

Pâtisserie Sobrie
Mageleinstraat 46–48
tel.: (09) 225 10 19

The Pâtisserie Sobrie is the place where the people of Gent come for really special *gâteaux*, *pâtisseries* and *tartes* as well as delicious Danish-style pastries. The most remarkable line, however, is the *pâtisseries* for slimmers, which look just as beautiful and enticing as all the others but, made with yoghurt and light lemon creams in place of rich cream and *crème fraîche*, remain delicious but are not fattening! The family also makes homemade ice creams and chocolates and there is an adjoining tea room where light, savoury lunches and sweet *pâtisseries* are served throughout the day. Daughter Tania Sobrie is an anglophile. Every year, she and her husband come to England for their annual holiday.

Pâtisserie Sobrie, Gent

Closed Tue., Sun. (lunchroom closed) and two weeks in Feb. ❖ English, French, Dutch and German spoken

This famous, old mustard shop in the Groentenmarkt is the oldest shop in the city still carrying on the same activity as when it was started. Founded in 1790 as a purveyor of spices and vinegar, the shop has been dispensing homemade Gent mustard since the early 1800s after soldiers in the service of Napoleon brought with them the secret of making Dijon-style mustard from finely ground mustard seeds, vinegar and salt. Today, mustard is still produced on the premises and locals come here with their own jars or pots to be filled from the huge mustard crock with a wooden ladle. This Gent mustard is sensational – fresh and nose-numbingly hot – and it is delicious served with local cheeses, pickles and beer. Come here to pick up paper-wrapped jars to take back home with you.

Closed Sun. ❖ English spoken

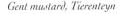

Gent mustard, Tierenteyn

Shopping for Food and Drink

CHEESE SHOP **Kaashandel Rogge** Groentenmarkt 16 tel.: (09) 225 20 15	Having purchased your jars of Gent mustard, make your way across the Groentenmarkt to Rogge's to choose from good selection of mainly Belgian cheeses to go with it. We think that the abbey cheeses such as those from Chimay or Orval are excellent with the mustard but young Michael Rogge, the fifth generation of the Rogge family to carry on the business here, will help you choose from nearly 250 different cheeses on offer. Try the Gent cheeses made with pepper and mustard, nettles, chives and celery or the traditional, unpasteurized Grand Cru. Michael keeps an impeccable selection of cheeses including French varieties from Philippe Olivier of Boulogne and a good choice of Dutch varieties. He also keeps a small selection of wines while his wife makes some superlative jams. Closed Sun. ❖ English spoken
GENT BISCUITS AND BREADS **Huis Van den Abeele** Meersenierstraat tel.: (09) 225 70 41	Come to this small shop by the bridge over the River Lys for typical Gent specialities such as *gentse mokken* (spicy, honey and anise cookies) and *pepperbollen* (cinammon, honey and pepper candies), as well as excellent local breads. *Pepperkoek*, for example, is a typical, spicy breakfast bread similar to French *pain d'épices* and dates back to the time when Flanders was part of the Burgundian Netherlands. Closed Sun., Mon.
GENT SPECIALITIES **Temmerman** Kraanlei 79 tel.: (09) 224 00 41	Madame Temmerman has a beautiful sweet shop located in one of the oldest houses on the Kraanlei, the House of the Works of Charity, built in the sixteenth century and decorated on the front with reliefs showing the works of the seven charities. Here she offers a selection of wonderful, handmade Gent specialities, candies and other sweets. 'I want to recreate for today's children the dreams and memories of my own childhood through the traditional sweets of Flanders,' she explained enthusiastically to us. Her sweets are, indeed, virtually works of art, packed by hand in beautiful bags sealed with hand-painted, plaster of Paris models. Come, then, to sample *bierbollen* (made with

Lindemann's *framboise* beer), *kriekspekken*, fruity *cuberdons*, *gentse mokken* and much else. These traditional, sometimes surprisingly spicy sweets are indeed a rather unusual taste of yesterday and may appeal as much to adults as to children!

Closed Sun.

Madame Temmerman, Gent

PÂTISSERIE
AND BAKERY

Pâtisserie Bloch
Veldstraat 60
Tel.: (09) 225 70 85

The Pâtisserie Bloch has been operating on the Veldstraat since 1898 with only a break during the last war when the Germans occupied the town. Mr Jacques Bloch remembers that as a young boy of just twelve years old, he was sent for safety to relatives in New York. When the family regrouped in 1945, they restarted the business, though the upstairs of the shop remained an English officer's mess until 1946. Today, the Pâtisserie Bloch is an outstanding bakery with an international outlook. There are yeast breads and *kugelhopfs* which demonstrate Alsace and Jewish traditions while a personal fondness for Britain means that there is an extensive range of traditional, British baked foods including versions of granary breads, scones, *bara brith*, even plum pudding. Moreover, during Mr Bloch's time in New York, he became particularly fond of heavy, New York style cheesecake and this can be found here, too, as well as New York style, deep-dish pizza. Recently, his son returned from the Middle East and developed ideas for a new type of

Turkish *brioche* made with sesame, and Israeli pastries made with chocolate and cinammon. Everything is freshly baked on the premises, and in the busy and popular lunchroom you can enjoy both light meals – shepherd's pie, lasagne, salads, pizza – as well as morning coffee or afternoon tea.

Closed Sun. ❖ English spoken

8970 POPERINGE (WEST FLANDERS) 🏛

Market   Fri.

Festival   International Hop Festival   every three years (next in 1996)

Calais 80 km – Ypres 12 km – Brugge 64 km

SPECIALIST
BEER SHOP

The Beer Store
Noël Cuvelier
Abelestationsplein 30
tel.: (057) 33 33 05

Just a few kilometres inside the Belgium border, farmer Noël Cuvelier has opened a remarkable and famous beer shop stocking some 300 different Belgian beers. Naturally, you can find the country's most famous beers here including Trappist ales (Chimay, Rochefort, Orval, and Westmalle); outstanding, strong ales like Duvel, Piraat, Kwak or the aptly-named Delerium Tremens; doubles and triples from Hoegaarden and Grimbergen; wheat beers; quenchingly sour, wood-aged beers like Rodenbach; lambics such as gueuze, kriek, framboise and faro; scotch ales; strong lager and much else. Many beers here are from small, artisan breweries and virtually unobtainable elsewhere. Noël himself makes frequent trips to the breweries themselves throughout the country to purchase his stock.

In addition to the beers, there is also an extensive collection of glasses for them. Noël himself is a real beer enthusiast and a member of CAMRA.

Closed Mon. ❖ English and French spoken

NATIONAL
HOP MUSEUM

**National Hop
Museum**
Stadsschaal
Gasthuisstraat 71

Located in the town, Stadsschaal, the National Hop Museum, parts of which date back to the sixteenth century, is a marvellously evocative example of industrial archaeology. As recently as 1968, the building was still used by the state for the processing of local hops for the Belgian brewing industry. Even today, the pungent, stingingly bitter, resinous aroma of dry hops permeates the very brick walls.

Come here to learn about the culture of hops, the social history of their cultivation, the necessary processing steps including drying in oast houses and pressing into tight pockets, their use in brewing and the marvellous, bitter palate and aroma that they give to beer. Rub the hop cones in your hands, smell them, imbibe the rare, aromatic

atmosphere of this historic building which, to beer lovers, houses what is, in essence, the very soul of beer. The tavern in the museum itself is sometimes open to individuals at the end of the tour. Otherwise, head for one of the town's many local bars and sample Poperinge's famous, quenchingly bitter and hoppy Hommelbier.

Open to individual visitors daily in July and Aug. 1430–1730; May and Sept. open Sun. and holidays only. The museum is closed from Nov.– mid-March

Hop gardens, Poperinge

---

640 WESTVLETEREN (WEST FLANDERS)

Calais 88 km – Poperinge 8 km – Brugge 63 km

RAPPIST BREWERY

bdij Sint-Sixtus

l.: (057) 40 10 57

Sint-Sixtus is one of the five great, genuine Trappist beers of Belgium. However, whereas all the others (Chimay, Orval, Westmalle, Rochefort) can generally be found in specialist beer shops as well as enjoyed in good beer taverns, Sint-Sixtus is a noncommercial brew that is usually only available at the abbey itself or in the bar across the road. This causes some confusion because about fifty years ago the abbey licensed the use of the Sint-Sixtus name to the St-Bernardus brewery in nearby Watou and, thus, a range of Sint-Sixtus abbey beers brewed commercially by St-Bernardus are widely available. Make no mistake, they are not the same thing! The beers as purchased at the Abdij Sint-Sixtus itself (always in plain, unlabelled bottles) are exactly the same as those which the thirty Trappist monks who still live and work in the abbey drink themselves: pure unfiltered, unpasteurized beers brewed according to ancient recipes with no addition of chemicals, additives or other skull-duggery as employed at other breweries which, perforce, must adopt commercial methods. 'Here we brew to live,' a monk told us simply, 'we do not live to brew.'

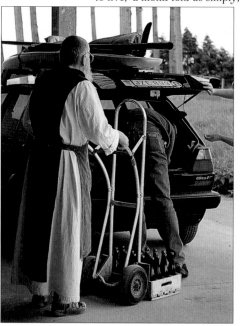

Abdij Sint-Sixtus, Westvleteren

Come to Westvleteren, then, first to sample at the café-bar across the road the three beers brewed at the abbey – Speciale 6° (red-cap), Extra 8° (blue-cap) and Abbot 12° (gold-cap) – then purchase them direct at the abbey itself where there is a unique and remarkable drive-in beer outlet. You drive your car into the loading bay, place your order with a Trappist monk who then loads your car with stamped, wooden crates of the unlabelled bottles of wondrous and delicious Sint-Sixtus Trappist beers. The abbey and the cafe-bar are the only places where genuine Sint-Sixtus can be purchased. The price for beer by the crate is extremely competitive (at the time of writing, Speciale is 550 BF per 24-bottle case, Extra is 670 BF per 24-bottle case and Abbot is 880 BF per 24-bottle case). You have to pay a small deposit for the lovely, wooden crates and unlabelled bottles, and the monk who runs the beer outlet will be very cross if you don't return them to the abbey on your next visit. 'The deposit doesn't even cover our costs,' he grumbled. 'Don't go telling everyone in Britain about us or we won't have any beer left for ourselves.'

Abbey beer sales open 1000–1200, 1400–1700. Closed Fri., Sun. and holidays, 1–14 Jan., one week after the third Sun. in Sept. Telephone in advance to ensure that beers are available as they are frequently sold out between July and Dec.
❖ English, French and German spoken

CAFÉ-BAR-BEER SHOP

In De Vrede
Donkerstraat 13

This café, bar and beer shop, located in front of the Abbey of Sint-Sixtus, is the only other authorized outlet for the sale of the Abbey's famous Trappist beers. Come here if you want to sample the Trappist beers with simple snacks, if you wish to purchase them in amounts of less than twenty-four bottles or if the abbey outlet itself is closed. However, the beers are more expensive here than at the abbey.

Closed Fri., first half of Jan. and second half of Sept. ❖ English spoken

INDEX OF PLACES AND ESTABLISHMENTS

Names of establishments appear in *italics*

Shopping for Food and Drink

COMMENT FORM

Please complete this form and let us know what you thought of the establishments you visited, irrespective of whether they appear in this guide. All the information that you send us will be used by Le Shuttle Guides to ensure that only the best places are recommended in future editions. Please photocopy this form if you want to comment on more than one establishment.

Name of establishment ....

Address ....

....

....

.... Post code ....

Telephone and/or fax number ....

Type of establishment

Hotel .... ☐   Restaurant .... ☐

Ferme auberge .... ☐   Chambre d'hôte .... ☐

Food or drink shop or outlet .... ☐

Date and duration of visit (if relevant) ....

Comment on existing entry .... ☐   New recommendation .... ☐

Comments (please describe whatever you think is relevant: food, drink, accommodation, service, personal welcome, noise, cleanliness, quality of produce/products, price, price/quality ratio). Please continue on a separate piece of paper if necessary.

....

....

....

....

....

....

....

....

....
....
....
....
....
....
....
....
....
....
....
....
....
....
....
....
....
....

Your name and address

Mr/Mrs/Miss/Ms/other .... Initials ....
Surname ....
Address ....
....
....
.... Post code ....

Please return your form to:

The Editor, Le Shuttle Travel Guides, Le Shuttle, FREEPOST RCC 2603,
Crawley, West Sussex, RH10 2ZA

No stamp is required if you post the letter in the UK. If you are mailing from
abroad, please add stamps at the appropriate rate.

We might like to publish your name and comments if you recommend a new
entry or support an existing one.
Please tick this box if you do not want your name to be used. .... ☐

As a matter of courtesy and business practice, Eurotunnel would like to keep you
informed about the services and offers the company and its marketing partners
may provide in the future.
If you would prefer not to receive this information, please tick this box. ..... ☐